CLASSICS IN EDUCATION
Lawrence A. Cremin, General Editor

☆　☆　☆

THE REPUBLIC AND THE SCHOOL
Horace Mann on the Education of Free Men
Edited by Lawrence A. Cremin

AMERICAN IDEAS ABOUT ADULT EDUCATION
1710–1951
Edited by C. Hartley Grattan

DEWEY ON EDUCATION
Introduction and Notes by Martin S. Dworkin

THE SUPREME COURT AND EDUCATION
Edited by David Fellman

INTERNATIONAL EDUCATION
A Documentary History
Edited by David G. Scanlon

CRUSADE AGAINST IGNORANCE
Thomas Jefferson on Education
Edited by Gordon C. Lee

CHINESE EDUCATION UNDER COMMUNISM
Edited by Chang-tu Hu

CHARLES W. ELIOT AND POPULAR EDUCATION
Edited by Edward A. Krug

WILLIAM T. HARRIS ON EDUCATION
(in preparation)
Edited by Martin S. Dworkin

THE *EMILE* OF JEAN JACQUES ROUSSEAU
Selections
Translated and Edited by William Boyd

THE MINOR EDUCATIONAL WRITINGS OF
JEAN JACQUES ROUSSEAU
Selected and Translated by William Boyd

PSYCHOLOGY AND THE SCIENCE OF EDUCATION
Selected Writings of Edward L. Thorndike
Edited by Geraldine M. Joncich

THE NEW-ENGLAND PRIMER
Introduction by Paul Leicester Ford

BENJAMIN FRANKLIN ON EDUCATION
Edited by John Hardin Best

THE COLLEGES AND THE PUBLIC
1787–1862
Edited by Theodore Rawson Crane

TRADITIONS OF AFRICAN EDUCATION
Edited by David G. Scanlon

NOAH WEBSTER'S AMERICAN SPELLING BOOK
Introductory Essay by Henry Steele Commager

VITTORINO DA FELTRE
AND OTHER HUMANIST EDUCATORS
by William Harrison Woodward
Foreword by Eugene F. Rice, Jr.

DESIDERIUS ERASMUS
CONCERNING THE AIM AND METHOD
OF EDUCATION
by William Harrison Woodward
Foreword by Craig R. Thompson

DEWEY ON EDUCATION

Selections

with an Introduction and Notes

by Martin S. Dworkin

CLASSICS IN

No. 3

EDUCATION

TEACHERS COLLEGE PRESS
TEACHERS COLLEGE, COLUMBIA UNIVERSITY
NEW YORK

The bust on the cover is by
Jacob Epstein. It is used
here with the kind permission of Mrs. John Dewey.

Printed in the United States of America

Contents

SERIES PREFACE

It seems the fate of every influential thinker to be much discussed but little read in the years immediately after his death. John Dewey is no exception. His writings have been translated into a dozen different languages; many are still in print; almost all are widely available. Yet contemporary educational discussion is filled with the shoddiest misconceptions of what he said; and disciples and critics alike have purveyed the grossest caricatures of his work. This volume, third in the *Classics in Education* series, ought to do much to clear the air. Mr. Dworkin has gathered together some of Dewey's clearest and most characteristic statements on education, and set them in the stream of American social and intellectual history. In addition, he has indicated some of the rich literature available to those who would probe more deeply into Dewey's ideas and the context in which they matured. Most important, perhaps, he has asked his readers neither to worship nor to damn Dewey, but rather to ponder him—which is, after all, what Dewey himself would most have appreciated.

Lawrence A. Cremin

John Dewey: A Centennial Review*

By Martin S. Dworkin

One hundred years after his birth, John Dewey is a figure of partisan fiction. Extreme disavowals of his importance are countered by passionate assertions of his greatness. Careful reappraisal of his work is itself ridiculed or ignored, either as part of a continuing conspiracy or as unnecessary annotation of explicit scriptures. The images of Dewey created in this kind of clamor may say a great deal about American attitudes at mid-century—as well as about traditional tendencies to view controversies as epic melodramas of heroes versus villains. But because Dewey played so consequential a part in American life, and had so profound an influence throughout the world, the fictitious figures of denied importance or affirmed greatness only block our view of the stage on which he moved and the drama in which he was a principal. Not only are we hindered in the necessary business of dealing with the many unclarities and unresolved difficulties of his work. We are prevented from seeing clearly the background of events and movements of ideas that we must rehearse and reexamine in order to know ourselves and the world in which we live.

Dewey's career was the longest among those philosophers for whom there are substantial and verifiable records. The range and quantity of his writings attest not merely his spirited activity until the very end of his life, but the astonishing vigor of the mind that was at work. His first publication, which appeared when he was

* An abridged version of this essay appeared in *School Executive*, Vol. 79, No. 2 (October 1959).

twenty-two, dealt with problems in metaphysics. The writings of his last fifteen years, which many professional philosophers regard as his weightiest contributions to the continuing philosophical dialogue, were concerned with logic, theory of value, methodology of the behavioral and physical sciences, and theory of knowledge. Problems of psychology, ethics, political science, jurisprudence, religion, and critical interpretation of movements and systems of thought were discussed in dozens of books and lectures, hundreds of articles for magazines, encyclopedias, specialized annuals, and other publications. Topical issues, ranging from election campaigns, the international drug traffic, birth control, pacifism, and the League of Nations to the revolutionary transformations of society in Mexico, China, Turkey, and Russia, were subjects of scores of pieces for periodicals and of numerous books.[1] But of all his published work, it is his writings on education that have exerted the widest and deepest influences upon life in the United States and other countries. And it is in the area of education that the question of his stature is presently most embattled and directly involved with issues which are among the most vital and urgent facing us today.

Irwin Edman remarked that it was "a historical accident that Dewey became widely known as an educator long before he became equally widely influential as a professional philosopher. That accident . . . conformed to Dewey's essential intent. . . ."[2] Edman's judgment of relative influences probably reflects a degree of wishful observation on the part of a professional philosopher. And we may well wonder at the meaning of an "acci-

[1] A bibliography of Dewey's published writings to October, 1939 is appended to *The Philosophy of John Dewey,* edited by Paul Arthur Schilpp (The Library of Living Philosophers, Volume I, Northwestern University, 1939; reprinted 1951, Tudor Publishing Company, New York). See also the successive editions of M. H. Thomas and Herbert W. Schneider, *A Bibliography of John Dewey, 1882-1939* (originally published by Columbia University Press in 1929; revised in 1939).

[2] Irwin Edman, *John Dewey* (Indianapolis: Bobbs-Merrill, 1955), p. 27.

dent" that is intentional. The paradox, at the least, that is suggested introduces the consideration of the place of Dewey's writings on education in the whole of his work. And this consideration leads further to the fundamental problem of the actual nature of his influence upon American education. To what extent, we must ask, was Dewey's impact unique, novel, truly innovative? And to what extent was it a product or expression of larger, ultimately determinant forces in American life? In dealing with these questions, more is involved than the inescapable task of understanding Dewey's work in order to criticize it. For Dewey's "responsibility" for the form and substance of American education has been one of the most persistent expletives of the bitter brawling over the schools, especially in the last decade. Was Dewey's influence accidental? Or was it inevitable? In either case, was it crucial?

We know far more about the background and development of Dewey's philosophy than we do about the context within which his educational ideas took on their power. One reason for this is surely the tendency in the genteel tradition of American scholarship to regard the study of education as worth no more than discreet afterthought. This attitude was attacked by Dewey himself as revealing a sadly inadequate understanding of what knowledge is, and an even sadder ignorance of how knowledge is to be made to benefit our lives. In fact, Dewey's gradual rejection of traditional philosophy took place during the period when he began to actively concern himself with problems of teaching and learning. It is a naive simplification to say, with many admirers and detractors of Dewey, that he broke with the tradition primarily or principally because of his emerging educational theories. What does appear reasonable, however, in the light of the influences bearing upon his early intellectual development, is that both his reaction against his own earlier philosophical training and his commitment to education were related in their origin.

Dewey began his philosophical studies, and did his first writing, during a period that Morton G. White drily describes as "no golden age of American philosophy."[3] Whatever philosophy there was in the colleges was usually closely tied to, and tied up in, theological studies. This association in large measure accounted for the dominance of the Scottish philosophy of common sense realism,[4] which reinforced religious faith against the tendencies toward doubt encouraged by the British empiricism it had supplanted. A strong surge of German idealism, derived particularly from Hegel and reinterpreted under the leadership of William Torrey Harris, was challenging proponents of the other schools.[5] The movement reflected the growing influence of the newly fashionable centers of learning in Germany, as well as the impressive scholarship and systematic ingenuity of the German philosophers.

The seemingly remote arguments over whether reality exists independently of sensation or consciousness had immediately urgent implications for questions relating to the authority of moral principles and the reasonableness

---

3 Morton G. White, *The Origin of Dewey's Instrumentalism* (New York: Columbia University Press, 1943), p. 3.

4 Founded by Thomas Reid (1710-1796), whose major works were *Enquiry into the Human Mind on the Principles of Common Sense* (London: 1764) and *Essays on the Intellectual Powers of Man* (Edinburgh: 1785), edited and abridged by A. D. Woozley (London: Macmillan, 1941). Historical studies of Scottish realism may be found in James McCosh, *The Scottish Philosophy* (New York: Robert Carter, 1874) and W. R. Sorley, *A History of English Philosophy*, Second Edition (Cambridge: 1937). A brief introduction is in the article "Scottish Philosophy," by William L. Davidson, in the *Encyclopedia of Religion and Ethics*, edited by James Hastings (Edinburgh: Clark, 1920), Vol. XI, pp. 261-271.

5 See the brief note, "William T. Harris and the Varieties of Idealism," in Morris R. Cohen, *American Thought: A Critical Sketch* (Glencoe, Illinois: Free Press, 1954), pp. 265-268. Harris, as Cohen remarks, "from 1867 to 1910 was regarded as the intellectual leader of the educational profession in the United States." His leadership of the Concord School of Philosophy, with Bronson Alcott, accomplished "the union of New England transcendentalism with Germanic scholarship and idealism." Perhaps the greatest single force of influence was *The Journal of Speculative Philosophy*, the first periodical in English devoted exclusively to philosophy, edited by Harris throughout its existence, from 1867 to 1893. Dewey's first writings appeared in the *Journal*.

of religious doctrine. But looming over the disputations was the enormous shadow of scientific discovery—particularly the mounting evidence for the theory of evolution and the striking, if often conflicting, findings of the new experimental psychologies.

At the University of Vermont, Dewey was exposed to Scottish realism in courses with H. A. P. Torrey. Later, in his graduate study at Johns Hopkins, he was profoundly affected by the Hegelian idealism of George Sylvester Morris[6]—an influence that continued when he joined the faculty of the University of Michigan, where Morris had become professor of philosophy. At Michigan, the first chair in education in the United States had already been established, and there were close relations between the faculty and the high schools of the state on matters of teacher preparation.

In the biographical essay prepared by Dewey's daughters with his assistance,[7] it is carefully noted that "his interest in general education was stimulated" by his participation in the program. This interest, to be sure, was more than theoretical. Before beginning his graduate work, he had taught "a little of everything" for two years at the high school at South Oil City, Pennsylvania, and later for a term in a village school at Charlotte, Vermont. The work with teachers and pupils at Michigan intensified his interest in psychology, which was grounded in his studies at Johns Hopkins with the pioneer of experimental psychology in the United States, G. Stanley Hall.

Dewey's first papers, lectures, and books for teachers dealt with psychology. In their orientation, they still reflected his philosophical idealism, notably in his postulation of a "universal consciousness" of which individual

6 See White, *op. cit.*, pp. 12-33. A comprehensive treatment of Morris, with bibliography, is Robert Mark Wenley, *The Life and Work of George Sylvester Morris* (New York: Macmillan, 1917). Introductions to Hegel include G. R. G. Mure, *An Introduction to Hegel* (Oxford: 1940), and W. T. Stace, *The Philosophy of Hegel* (London: Macmillan, 1923; reprinted Dover, New York, 1955).

7 "Biography of John Dewey," edited by Jane M. Dewey. In Schilpp, *op. cit.*, pp. 3-45.

knowledge is a kind of special case. But the experimental basis of the new psychology, and the way it seemed to bring human behavior into the natural order in accordance with evolutionary theory, was making a profound impression upon Dewey, as upon the whole of higher learning in the United States. The most significant single influence unquestionably was the thought of William James. James's *Principles of Psychology,* published in 1890,[8] clearly illustrates the association of the new experimental outlook with evolutionary theory in the foundation of American pragmatic philosophy.[9]

Other major influences were the social behaviorism of George Herbert Mead[10] and the economic sociology of Thorstein Veblen.[11] With Veblen, Dewey was influenced by Marx but more closely by the militant reformism of the "muckraker" journalists: Lincoln Steffens, Ida M. Tarbell, Jacob Riis, Upton Sinclair, and others. These influences affected the development of Dewey's own form of pragmatism. Moving from the more restrictively philosophical enterprise of William James and Charles Sanders Peirce, Dewey came to place that emphasis upon social purposes and political action that is inherent in what he came to term his "experimentalism," and, later, "instrumentalism."

Dewey's central concept of "experience," by which he

8 New York: Henry Holt & Company.

9 On this relationship see especially Philip P. Wiener, *Evolution and the Founders of Pragmatism* (Cambridge: Harvard University Press, 1949) and Stow Persons, editor, *Evolutionary Thought in America* (New Haven: Yale University Press, 1950).

10 See George H. Mead, *Mind, Self, and Society* (Chicago: University of Chicago Press, 1934); "The Genesis of the Self and Social Control," *International Journal of Ethics,* Vol. XXXV (1924-25), pp. 251-77; "A Pragmatic Theory of Truth," *Studies in the Nature of Truth, University of California Publications in Philosophy,* Vol. XI (1929), pp. 65-88. For studies of Mead's influence, see Alfred S. Clayton, *Emergent Mind and Education* (New York: Bureau of Publications, Teachers College, Columbia University, 1943); also Charles W. Morris, "Peirce, Mead and Pragmatism," *Philosophical Review,* Vol. XLVII (1938), pp. 109-27.

11 See particularly Veblen's *The Theory of the Leisure Class* (New York: Macmillan, 1899) and *The Higher Learning in America* (New York: Huebsch, 1918).

claimed to have avoided dualistic distinctions of perception and objective reality, is essentially one of a social process. And the "method of intelligence," which he argued as the governor of experience, is most truly practiced and fulfilled in application to social and political affairs—the area in which education is the most important instrument of action. In general, the direction of Dewey's thinking was away from the idea of philosophy as an academic discipline removed from immediate involvement in human affairs, toward that insistence upon action implied in the famous definition of philosophy, in *Democracy and Education,* as "the theory of education as a deliberately conducted practice."[12]

The changes in Dewey's thinking are one evidence of how deeply the scientific and intellectual movements of the time were involved in volcanic turbulences in American life. This was a period of national consolidation following civil war. The expanding nation was overflowing the continental frontiers to gather in new territories and responsibilities, while the population grew explosively as multitudes of immigrants continued to pour into the country. It was a time of accelerating innovation in technology—along with the growth of industrial complexes of such gigantic size and pervasive power as had never been seen before on earth. In rural, agricultural America, life was being transformed by railroads and farm machinery. In urban, industrial and commercial America, traditional ways of family living and the still immature political institutions of the young democracy were being confronted by strange, often terrifying, problems. Throughout the country, forces for social and political reform were working to organize farmers and industrial laborers, or striving to arouse the interest and the conscience of the propertied, professional, and commercial classes.

The coming together, in the 1880s and 1890s, of the evolutionary approach in the natural sciences, experimental method in the social sciences, and pragmatism in

12 *Democracy and Education* (New York: The Macmillan Company, 1916), p. 387.

philosophy—in a world of technological transformation
and in an atmosphere of social and political reformism
—could not fail to have consequences in education. The
effect would have been the same even if the schools
themselves had not been in their usual need of change.
Dewey's arrival at the University of Chicago in 1894 as
head of the department of philosophy, psychology, and
pedagogy, may truly be one of the most decisive events
in American education. In historical importance, it may
be compared, perhaps, only to the accession of Horace
Mann in 1837 to the secretaryship of the Massachusetts
State Board of Education, where he proceeded to develop and promote the idea of the common or public
school. In the Laboratory School which Dewey founded
in 1896 with Mrs. Alice Chipman Dewey, the basic ideas
of progressive education were experimentally worked
out.[13] These ideas were spread throughout America and
the world by his teaching and articles and books such
as *My Pedagogic Creed*,[14] *The School and Society*,[15] and
The Child and the Curriculum,[16] all included in this
volume, and, later, *Schools of To-Morrow* (with Evelyn
Dewey),[17] *Democracy and Education*,[18] and *Experience
and Education*.[19]

But the Laboratory School, as is being substantiated in
the researches of Ray Ginger[20] and Robert L. McCaul,[21]

[13] The fullest account of the Laboratory School is in Katherine
Camp Mayhew and Anna Camp Edwards, *The Dewey School* (New
York: Appleton-Century, 1936). A study of the theoretical back-
ground of the work of the school is Melvin C. Baker's *Foundations
of John Dewey's Educational Theory* (New York: King's Crown
Press, 1955).

[14] First published as Number IX in a series under the title, in
The School Journal, Vol. LIV, No. 3 (January 16, 1897), pp. 77-80.

[15] Chicago: University of Chicago Press, 1899.

[16] Chicago: University of Chicago Press, 1902.

[17] New York: Dutton, 1915.

[18] *Op. cit.*

[19] New York: Macmillan, 1938.

[20] Ray Ginger, *Altgeld's America* (New York: Funk & Wagnalls
Company, 1958).

[21] Robert L. McCaul, "Dewey's Chicago," *The School Review*,
Vol. LXVII (1959), pp. 258-280.

was in one sense a single phenomenon of a complex of reform movements in and around Chicago—including the famous settlement house project of Jane Addams and the experimental school of Francis W. Parker. And the whole progressive education movement, which Dewey is sometimes supposed to have begun and promoted single handed, is being shown in the work of Lawrence A. Cremin to have been but one factor in a nationwide, comprehensive reform movement: "In the universities it appeared as part of a spirited revolt against formalism in philosophy, psychology, and the social sciences. In the cities it emerged as one facet of a larger program of social alleviation and municipal reform. Among farmers, it became the crux of a moderate, liberal alternative to radical agrarianism."[22]

In education, progressivism brought together several familiar tendencies—but with contemporary modifications. One tendency was a romantic emphasis upon the needs and interests of the child, in the tradition of Rousseau, Pestalozzi, and Froebel—but now colored and given scientific authority by the new psychology of learning and behavior. Another was the democratic faith in the instrument of the common, or public school, inherited from Jefferson and Mann—but now applied to the problems of training the urban and rural citizenry for industrial and agricultural vocations, and of acculturating or Americanizing the swelling masses of immigrants. By the time Dewey moved to Columbia University in 1904, he was truly the leading theoretician and spokesman of the movement. But his leadership then—and, indeed, from then on—was largely that of a reverently misinterpreted prophet rather than of a carefully obeyed commander.

In the courses he gave at Teachers College, in addition to his work in Columbia's graduate faculty of philosophy, Dewey directly influenced tens of thousands of students from all over the world. Teachers—and the public—throughout the nation were affected by

22 Lawrence A. Cremin, "John Dewey and the Progressive Education Movement, 1915-1952," *The School Review, ibid.*, p. 160.

his activities in promoting teaching as a profession, by his involvement in politics, and by his work in helping to form the first unions of teachers in the United States: the American Association of University Professors and the New York Teachers Union, later to become part of the American Federation of Teachers. What his myriads of disciples and opponents did not seem to take seriously at the time, however, was his mounting criticism of the educational movement of which he was "leader."

It is significant that he repeatedly refused to associate himself with the Progressive Education Association, founded in 1919—only consenting much later on to acclamation as honorary president. During the 1920s, and increasingly in the '30s and '40s, Dewey voiced his doubts about what he considered extremist or romantic oversimplifications in the movement. In the address, "Progressive Education and the Science of Education,"[23] which is reprinted here, Dewey spoke of the end of "the earlier and more negative phase of progressive education," outlining the need for rigor and clarity, for consideration of "the intellectual contribution which it may make to the art of education." He sharply warned against the aimlessness and dangerous permissiveness of the notion of "the child centered school," with its mixture of post-war bohemianism, undisciplined expression in the name of individual creativity, and Freudian solicitude for avoiding inhibitions. Later, while participating in the projection of progressivism into politics with the Social Frontier group, he carefully denied the practicality or desirability of using the schools to "remake the social order," as advocated by George Counts and others. He frequently complained about what he considered evasions of educational responsibility in many so-called "progressive" schools. Subject matter, for example, too often had been eliminated or minimized, when the truly progressive approach called for recreating the curriculum to develop new subject matter. The ideas of adjustment and free expression, too, had been exaggerated

23 *Progressive Education*, Vol. V, (1928), pp. 197-204.

and even perverted, wherever the schools did not promote an actively critical attitude toward society.

Dewey objected to attempts to associate progressivism with Communism. His jaundiced reports of his observations in Soviet Russia in 1928[24] included criticism of how some of his ideas supposedly had been put into practice there. In many ways, his participation in the Commission of Inquiry that went to Mexico in 1937, to investigate the charges made against Leon Trotsky at the Moscow trials, may be seen as being in the same vein of warning progressives and liberals generally against excesses or corruptions of their beliefs.[25]

Some of Dewey's later work in philosophy was ignored by many of his most ardent followers, particularly in education, while attracting serious study by others who had not taken him seriously before precisely because of his concern with education. Dewey had found the atmosphere at Columbia quite different from that at Chicago. In particular, the historically grounded Aristotelian realism of Frederick J. E. Woodbridge led, as Jane Dewey notes, "to a rethinking of all his philosophic ideas."[26] In his teaching in the graduate faculty, and in books such as *Reconstruction in Philosophy*,[27] *Experience and Nature*,[28] and *The Quest for Certainty*,[29] he

24 Dewey's articles on Soviet Russia published during 1928 in *The New Republic* were collected in *Impressions of Soviet Russia and the Revolutionary World, Mexico–China–Turkey* (New York: New Republic, 1929). Also see: "Why I Am Not a Communist," in *The Meaning of Marx, A Symposium*, by Bertrand Russell, John Dewey, and others (New York: Farrar & Rinehart, 1934).

25 See *The Case of Leon Trotsky; Report of Hearings on the Charges Made Against Him in The Moscow Trials*, by the Preliminary Commission of Inquiry, John Dewey, Chairman (New York: Harper, 1937), and *Not Guilty: Report of the Commission of Inquiry Into the Charges Made Against Leon Trotsky in the Moscow Trials*, John Dewey, Chairman (New York: Harper, 1938).

26 "Biography of John Dewey," *op. cit.*, p. 36. Woodbridge's principal works are *The Realm of Mind* (New York: Columbia, 1926), *Nature and Mind* (New York: Columbia, 1937), *An Essay on Nature* (New York: Columbia, 1940).

27 New York: Holt, 1920.

28 Lectures Upon the Paul Carus Foundation, First Series (Chicago: Open Court, 1925).

29 Gifford Lectures (New York: Minton, Balch, 1929).

felt compelled to contend with problems of traditional metaphysical philosophy that had seemed to have been successfully eliminated in the first brilliance of pragmatism.[30]

This contention continued in the major works of his later years, including *Art as Experience*,[31] *Logic: The Theory of Inquiry*,[32] *Theory of Valuation*,[33] and his last book, with Arthur F. Bentley, *Knowing and the Known*.[34] It was in this period that he stated, in *A Common Faith*,[35] the principles of a religion of "shared experience" and of "scientific humanism" that he believed could supplant traditional faiths having their historical origins in prescientific ignorance. Until the very end of his life, Dewey was engaged in vigorous exposition and defense of his ideas. He continued to write articles for magazines, and was indefatigable in providing forewords and introductions to books in the many areas of his interest. His last published work on education, in fact, was the Introduction to Elsie Ripley Clapp's *The Use of Resources in Education*,[36] which is reprinted in this volume. Dewey continued his extensive correspondence with friends, former students, and many of the leading men of ideas of the world. One important, still-unpublished body of letters, for example, comprises a discussion with Bentley and Felix Kaufmann that was going on at the

30 During this period, Dewey revised two of his most influential textbooks in philosophy and psychology: *Ethics* (with James H. Tufts) (New York: Holt, 1908; rev. ed. 1932); and *How We Think* (New York: Heath, 1910; rev. ed. 1933). He also published his chief works on social psychology: *Human Nature and Conduct* (New York: Holt, 1922; reprinted with a new foreword by The Modern Library, New York, 1930); and political philosophy: *The Public and Its Problems* (New York: Holt, 1927; reprinted with a new introduction by Gateway Books, Chicago, 1946).

31 New York: Minton, Balch, 1934.

32 New York: Holt, 1938.

33 University of Chicago Press, *International Encyclopedia of Unified Science*, Vol. II, No. 4, 1939.

34 Boston: Beacon, 1949.

35 New Haven: Yale University Press, 1934.

36 Published for The John Dewey Society by Harper, New York, 1952.

time of his death. The letters treat in detail many fundamental problems of methodology and theory of knowledge, notably those raised by his proposal of a concept of "warranted assertibility" in place of traditional measures of "truth," and by the term "transaction," with which he and Bentley sought to eliminate the duality of knower and known, elaborating and clarifying much of what he had earlier intended by the term "experience."

Dewey's language, indeed, is a principal factor in the persistent problems of measuring the·effects of his work against his intentions, and of distinguishing the latter from the interpretations of his disciples. Dewey wrote badly. His style was often opaque, his terminology ambiguous. In his writing on technical problems of philosophy, it is true that he was attempting to express antidualistic reasoning in language traditionally and inherently dualistic. But therein lies one of the most serious difficulties of his entire work. The problem of his language is inextricable from the problem of his philosophy, quite apart from the infelicities of his style.[37]

Critics have long complained, for example, about the vagueness of his central terms, "experience" and "inquiry," by which he intended to indicate an essential unity of experienc*er* and experienc*ed,* of inquirer and problematic situation, without an idea of an observing mind or consciousness. Dewey's language, if not his intention, has been said to cause the individual inquirer to vanish into the situation, or into the social group, with only a trace of purpose to mark his existence. Even more complaints have been made about the ambiguity of Dewey's meaning of "growth" as an end in itself. The dictum that education ought to lead only to more education, growth to more growth, has been criticised as without precise meaning at best and as a justification of aimlessness at worst. In a way, Dewey may be said to deserve

37 For a discussion of the relation of Dewey's language to his theory of language, see Emmanuel G. Mesthene, "The Role of Language in the Philosophy of John Dewey," *Philosophy and Phenomenological Research,* University of Buffalo, Vol. XIX, No. 4, June, 1959, pp. 511-517.

whatever confusions came to be associated with his name. It may be no compliment to professional educators that they so easily understood Dewey while philosophers shook their heads.[38]

Dewey's writing, as Felix Kaufmann once remarked about the *Logic*, "is like a witch's mirror in which every man may see his sweetheart—or the devil."[39] Dewey's followers have continually bickered among themselves over their certainties about his meaning. His opponents have blamed what Eliseo Vivas, with typical restraint, has called his "menticidal obscenities"[40] for every fault of American life of the past half-century—and especially for the crisis in education. Dewey himself complained that many of his followers—and especially among educators—either did not understand his work or garbled just enough to use for their own purposes. In one sense, the dangers of misinterpretation were inherent in Dewey's prescription of experimental action. His conception of the discipline of philosophy as the generalization of educational theory appealed directly to a hallowed American reluctance to theorize. Here seemed to be a way to philosophize by *doing,* rather than by thinking only. Of course, the hard work of conventional thinking was vital, but in the massive scriptures of the prophet most of it had already been done. The educator would be the philosopher thinking aloud, and his "thoughts" would be the actual experiences of the children in the schools. Society would be a vast mind engaged in endless experiment, and its "ideas" would be

38 A penetrating critique of Dewey's general philosophical position is by Morris R. Cohen, "Some Difficulties in John Dewey's Anthropocentric Naturalism," *The Philosophical Review,* Vol. XLIX, 1940; reprinted in Morris R. Cohen, *Studies In Philosophy and Science* (New York: Holt, 1949), pp. 139-175. Other critical views, with a general reply by Dewey, "Experience, Knowledge and Value: A Rejoinder," may be found in Schilpp, *op. cit.*

39 Felix Kaufmann, "John Dewey's Theory of Inquiry," in *John Dewey: Philosopher of Science and Freedom,* a Symposium edited by Sidney Hook (New York: Dial, 1950), page 230.

40 Letter, "To the Editor," *National Review,* New York, Vol. VI, No. 15, December 20, 1958, page 413.

the events in their chain of trial, error, and inexorable progress.

Dewey suffered his own chagrin at being taken up by acolytes of good intentions whom Russell Kirk has referred to as "that distraught crowd of the semi-educated."[41] But he did not assist the completion of their education, in at least one crucial ambiguity in his thinking. He is continually ambivalent on the basic intellectual issue of the value of traditional knowledge. Sometimes a single article is truly a "witch's mirror" wherein we see reflections of two faces: the one demanding study of history and of the learning of the past as vital for understanding of the present; the other calling for liberation from all old ideas and knowledge, in order to be untrammeled in developing new ideas and knowledge.

Here, of course, are the horns of the dilemma of the reformer in all ages. And it is not disparagement to say that Dewey's indecision is infinitely preferable to the certainties of censors and commissars, obliterating the past in order to control the present in the name of some future. But wherever Dewey appears to argue against study of the past, he is raising up the two worst enemies of his true enterprise and his reputation. On the one hand, there arise the epigones, the blind believers who are absolved of the necessity of gaining the background to criticize his work, and hence can never understand what they believe or control what they practice. On the other, there are those made into implacable enemies by his apparent vandalism in the temples of civilization. Because so often he seems to repudiate perspective in the name of progress, he prevents both groups from viewing him in perspective—and makes the task of judging his work and influence difficult and thankless.

It is a century since John Dewey was born, but still hardly a decade since his death. We are only beginning the kind of critical examination of his ideas and his

41 Russell Kirk, *The Conservative Mind* (Chicago: Regnery, 1953), p. 365.

times that will reveal his impact upon our ideas and our times. A great deal of material remains to be collected and published. As yet, there are only a handful of comprehensive critical studies, and there is no biography that is more than a sketchy résumé.[42] But a few tentative judgments can be made, seeking something beyond the way he is uncritically revered by some or the way he is cited without being read, and refuted without being understood, by others, who can explain evils only by placing blame.

Dewey's place in the history of thought may be quite different from that assigned to him at present by his admirers and detractors. But that he does have a place, and an important one, is deniable only by those to whom history and logic are irrelevant. His contribution may be less innovation than synthesis; his true uniqueness more an encyclopedic range over problems of thought and conduct than any particular nuance of expression. When the University of Paris conferred an

---

[42] Collections made by Dewey himself of his essays and addresses include: *The Influence of Darwin on Philosophy and Other Essays in Contemporary Thought* (New York: Holt, 1910); *Essays in Experimental Logic* (Chicago: University of Chicago Press, 1916; reprinted 1954, by Dover Publications, Inc., New York); *Philosophy and Civilization* (New York: Minton, Balch, 1931); and *Problems of Men* (New York: Philosophical Library, 1946).

Collections by others, with introductory materials, of Dewey's essays and addresses include: *Characters and Events,* edited by Joseph Ratner, two volumes (New York: Holt, 1929); *Intelligence in the Modern World: John Dewey's Philosophy,* edited by Joseph Ratner (New York: Modern Library, 1939); and Irwin Edman, *op. cit.*

Collections of essays in honor of or about Dewey, in addition to those cited above, include: *Essays in Honor of John Dewey on the Occasion of His Seventieth Birthday* (New York: Holt, 1929); *The Philosopher of the Common Man: Essays in Honor of John Dewey to Celebrate His Eightieth Birthday,* edited by Sidney Ratner (New York: G. P. Putnam's Sons, 1940).

General and introductory studies include: Sidney Hook, *John Dewey: An Intellectual Portrait* (New York: John Day, 1939); Jerome Nathanson, *John Dewey, The Reconstruction of the Democratic Life* (New York: Scribner's, 1951); and George R. Geiger, *John Dewey in Perspective* (New York: Oxford University Press, 1958).

honorary degree upon him in 1930, the citation described him as "the most profound and complete expression of American genius." The French scholars, led by Emile Durkheim, were not being invidious, but were paying tribute to the grandeur with which Dewey had embodied and expressed the movements of ideas, the pioneering experiences, and the progressive aspirations of the new country. It is academic whether Dewey is the best among the best American philosophers: Charles S. Peirce, William James, Josiah Royce, Morris Raphael Cohen, George Santayana. If we ask, however, about the degree to which our lives are different because of a man's career, Dewey is unquestionably the most important.

Dewey's impact upon American life, however, must be carefully evaluated with regard to the forces that were at work. The deepest meaning of the need to distinguish Dewey from his followers in progressive education, and to limit his responsibility for practices committed in his name, may lie in the essential nature of what we call "progressivism." The many elements of that complex movement of thought and action may turn out to have had their own origins and momentums, working out their own courses toward their own outcomes. For one extended instant in history, those elements or forces may be said to have converged and focused in Dewey's work. When in time they diverged and passed on, the philosopher was left to chide and criticize, warning of dangers and reconsidering and reformulating his ideas. Dewey gathered, rearranged, and recreated elements of educational reform that had been at work for decades—and even centuries. Even his experiments may be said to have been superbly appropriate—as punctually conceived and performed as if he had had an eye on a clock of destiny. Dewey the instrumentalist may have been as much an instrument of forces in American history and society as he was their organizer and shaper. It may make more sense to hold the American people responsible for what they made of Dewey than to condemn his villainy in coming to lead so many who were waiting and willing.

In writing of "Philosophy and Civilization," Dewey reflected that "Philosophies which emerge at distinctive periods define the larger patterns of continuity which are woven in effecting the enduring junctions of a stubborn past and an insistent future."[43] After all the critiques of faults and unclarities, and the presentments of excesses and distortions, there remains what may be the truest measure of John Dewey's career: that without understanding it, we cannot understand our history, our present, and the directions toward our future.

[43] In *Philosophy and Civilization, op. cit.,* page 7.

My Pedagogic Creed *

---◆---

Among the hundreds of books, essays, and other works Dewey produced in his long career, the educational credo he wrote in 1897 is uniquely significant. In its style and content, it may most clearly exemplify the reformist fervor of his Chicago period. Here is Dewey passionately, even flamboyantly, confident of his vision of the nature, purpose, and inevitable progress of education. At once a personal declaration and a revolutionary manifesto, it dispenses with supporting arguments or documentation. The resulting clarity, succinctness, and even eloquence have offered incomparable opportunities for interpretation, to both disciples and critics.

ARTICLE I—What Education Is

I believe that all education proceeds by the participation of the individual in the social consciousness of the race. This process begins unconsciously almost at birth, and is continually shaping the individual's powers, saturating his consciousness, forming his habits, training his ideas, and arousing his feelings and emotions. Through this unconscious education the individual gradually comes to share in the intellectual and moral resources which humanity has succeeded in getting together. He becomes an inheritor of the funded capital of civilization. The most formal and technical education in the world can-

---

* Number IX in a series under this title, in *The School Journal*, Vol. LIV, No. 3 (January 16, 1897), pp. 77-80.

not safely depart from this general process. It can only organize it or differentiate it in some particular direction.

I believe that the only true education comes through the stimulation of the child's powers by the demands of the social situations in which he finds himself. Through these demands he is stimulated to act as a member of a unity, to emerge from his original narrowness of action and feeling, and to conceive of himself from the standpoint of the welfare of the group to which he belongs. Through the responses which others make to his own activities he comes to know what these mean in social terms. The value which they have is reflected back into them. For instance, through the response which is made to the child's instinctive babblings the child comes to know what those babblings mean; they are transformed into articulate language and thus the child is introduced into the consolidated wealth of ideas and emotions which are now summed up in language.

I believe that this educational process has two sides— one psychological and one sociological; and that neither can be subordinated to the other or neglected without evil results following. Of these two sides, the psychological is the basis. The child's own instincts and powers furnish the material and give the starting point for all education. Save as the efforts of the educator connect with some activity which the child is carrying on of his own initiative independent of the educator, education becomes reduced to a pressure from without. It may, indeed, give certain external results, but cannot truly be called educative. Without insight into the psychological structure and activities of the individual, the educative process will, therefore, be haphazard and arbitrary. If it chances to coincide with the child's activity it will get a leverage; if it does not, it will result in friction, or disintegration, or arrest of the child nature.

I believe that knowledge of social conditions, of the present state of civilization, is necessary in order properly to interpret the child's powers. The child has his own instincts and tendencies, but we do not know what these mean until we can translate them into their social equivalents. We must be able to carry them back into a social past and see them as the inheritance of previous race activities. We must also be able to project them into the future to see what their outcome and end will be. In the illustration just used, it is the ability to see in the child's babblings the promise and potency of a future social intercourse and conversation which enables one to deal in the proper way with that instinct.

I believe that the psychological and social sides are organically related and that education cannot be regarded as a compromise between the two, or a superimposition of one upon the other. We are told that the psychological definition of education is barren and formal—that it gives us only the idea of a development of all the mental powers without giving us any idea of the use to which these powers are put. On the other hand, it is urged that the social definition of education, as getting adjusted to civilization, makes of it a forced and external process, and results in subordinating the freedom of the individual to a preconceived social and political status.

I believe that each of these objections is true when urged against one side isolated from the other. In order to know what a power really is we must know what its end, use, or function is; and this we cannot know save as we conceive of the individual as active in social relationships. But, on the other hand, the only possible adjustment which we can give to the child under existing conditions, is that which arises through putting him in complete possession of all his powers. With the advent of democracy and modern industrial conditions, it is impossible to foretell definitely just what civilization will be twenty years from now. Hence it is impossible to prepare the child for any precise set of conditions. To prepare him for the future life means to give him command of himself; it means so to train him that he will have the full and ready use of all his capacities; that his eye and ear and hand may be tools ready to command, that his judgment may be capable of grasping the conditions under which it has to work, and the executive forces be trained to act economically and efficiently. It is impossible to reach this sort of adjustment save as constant regard is had to the individual's own powers, tastes, and interests—say, that is, as education is continually converted into psychological terms.

In sum, I believe that the individual who is to be educated is a social individual and that society is an organic union of individuals. If we eliminate the social factor from the child we are left only with an abstraction; if we eliminate the individual factor from society, we are left only with an inert and lifeless mass. Education, therefore, must begin with a psychological insight into the child's capacities, interests, and habits. It must be controlled at every point by reference to these same considerations. These powers, interests, and habits must be continually interpreted—we must know what they mean. They must be translated into terms of their social equivalents—into terms of what they are capable of in the way of social service.

ARTICLE II—What the School Is

I believe that the school is primarily a social institution. Education being a social process, the school is simply that form of community life in which all those agencies are concentrated that will be most effective in bringing the child to share in the inherited resources of the race, and to use his own powers for social ends.

I believe that education, therefore, is a process of living and not a preparation for future living.

I believe that the school must represent present life—life as real and vital to the child as that which he carries on in the home, in the neighborhood, or on the playground.

I believe that education which does not occur through forms of life, or that are worth living for their own sake, is always a poor substitute for the genuine reality and tends to cramp and to deaden.

I believe that the school, as an institution, should simplify existing social life; should reduce it, as it were, to an embryonic form. Existing life is so complex that the child cannot be brought into contact with it without either confusion or distraction; he is either overwhelmed by the multiplicity of activities which are going on, so that he loses his own power of orderly reaction, or he is so stimulated by these various activities that his powers are prematurely called into play and he becomes either unduly specialized or else disintegrated.

I believe that as such simplified social life, the school life should grow gradually out of the home life; that it should take up and continue the activities with which the child is already familiar in the home.

I believe that it should exhibit these activities to the child, and reproduce them in such ways that the child will gradually learn the meaning of them, and be capable of playing his own part in relation to them.

I believe that this is a psychological necessity, because it is the only way of securing continuity in the child's growth, the only way of giving a back-ground of past experience to the new ideas given in school.

I believe that it is also a social necessity because the home is the form of social life in which the child has been nurtured and in connection with which he has had his moral training. It is the business of the school to deepen and extend his sense of the values bound up in his home life.

I believe that much of present education fails because it neglects this fundamental principle of the school as a form of community life. It conceives the school as a place where certain information is to be given, where certain lessons are to be learned, or where certain habits are to be formed. The value of these is conceived as lying largely in the remote future; the child must do these things for the sake of something else he is to do; they are mere preparation. As a result they do not become a part of the life experience of the child and so are not truly educative.

I believe that the moral education centers upon this conception of the school as a mode of social life, that the best and deepest moral training is precisely that which one gets through having to enter into proper relations with others in a unity of work and thought. The present educational systems, so far as they destroy or neglect this unity, render it difficult or impossible to get any genuine, regular moral training.

I believe that the child should be stimulated and controlled in his work through the life of the community.

I believe that under existing conditions far too much of the stimulus and control proceeds from the teacher, because of neglect of the idea of the school as a form of social life.

I believe that the teacher's place and work in the school is to be interpreted from this same basis. The teacher is not in the school to impose certain ideas or to form certain habits in the child, but is there as a member of the community to select the influences which shall affect the child and to assist him in properly responding to these influences.

I believe that the discipline of the school should proceed from the life of the school as a whole and not directly from the teacher.

I believe that the teacher's business is simply to determine on the basis of larger experience and riper wisdom, how the discipline of life shall come to the child.

I believe that all questions of the grading of the child and his promotion should be determined by reference to the same standard. Examinations are of use only so far as they test the child's fitness for social life and reveal the place in which he can be of the most service and where he can receive the most help.

ARTICLE III—The Subject-Matter of Education

I believe that the social life of the child is the basis of concentration, or correlation, in all his training or growth. The social life gives the unconscious unity and the background of all his efforts and of all his attainments.

I believe that the subject-matter of the school curriculum should mark a gradual differentiation out of the primitive unconscious unity of social life.

I believe that we violate the child's nature and render difficult the best ethical results, by introducing the child too abruptly to a number of special studies, of reading, writing, geography, etc., out of relation to this social life.

I believe, therefore, that the true center of correlation on the school subjects is not science, nor literature, nor history, nor geography, but the child's own social activities.

I believe that education cannot be unified in the study of science, or so called nature study, because apart from human activity, nature itself is not a unity; nature in itself is a number of diverse objects in space and time, and to attempt to make it the center of work by itself, is to introduce a principle of radiation rather than one of concentration.

I believe that literature is the reflex expression and interpretation of social experience; that hence it must follow upon and not precede such experience. It, therefore, cannot be made the basis, although it may be made the summary of unification.

I believe once more that history is of educative value in so far as it presents phases of social life and growth. It must be controlled by reference to social life. When taken simply as history it is thrown into the distant past and becomes dead and inert. Taken as the record of man's social life and progress it becomes full of meaning. I believe, however, that it cannot be so taken excepting as the child is also introduced directly into social life.

I believe accordingly that the primary basis of education is in the child's powers at work along the same general constructive lines as those which have brought civilization into being.

I believe that the only way to make the child conscious of his social heritage is to enable him to perform those fundamental types of activity which make civilization what it is.

I believe, therefore, in the so-called expressive or constructive activities as the center of correlation.

I believe that this gives the standard for the place of cooking, sewing, manual training, etc., in the school.

I believe that they are not special studies which are to be introduced over and above a lot of others in the way of relaxation or relief, or as additional accomplishments. I believe rather that they represent, as types, fundamental forms of social activity; and that it is possible and desirable that the child's introduction into the more formal subjects of the curriculum be through the medium of these activities.

I believe that the study of science is educational in so far as it brings out the materials and processes which make social life what it is.

I believe that one of the greatest difficulties in the present teaching of science is that the material is presented in purely objective form, or is treated as a new peculiar kind of experience which the child can add to that which he has already had. In reality, science is of value because it gives the ability to interpret and control the experience already had. It should be introduced, not as so much new subject-matter, but as showing the factors already involved in previous experience and as furnishing tools by which that experience can be more easily and effectively regulated.

I believe that at present we lose much of the value of literature and language studies because of our elimination of the social element. Language is almost always treated in the books of pedagogy simply as the expression of thought. It is true that language is a logical instrument, but it is fundamentally and primarily a social instrument. Language is the device for communication; it is the tool through which one individual comes to share the ideas and feelings of others. When treated simply as a way of getting individual information, or as a means of showing off what one has learned, it loses its social motive and end.

I believe that there is, therefore, no succession of studies in the ideal school curriculum. If education is life, all life has, from the outset, a scientific aspect, an aspect of art and culture, and an aspect of communication. It cannot, therefore, be true that the proper studies for one grade are mere reading and writing, and that at a later grade, reading, or literature, or science, may be introduced. The progress is not in the succession of studies but in the development of new attitudes towards, and new interests in, experience.

I believe finally, that education must be conceived as a continuing reconstruction of experience; that the process and the goal of education are one and the same thing.

I believe that to set up any end outside of education, as furnishing its goal and standard, is to deprive the educational process of much of its meaning and tends to make us rely upon false and external stimuli in dealing with the child.

Article IV—The Nature of Method

I believe that the question of method is ultimately reducible to the question of the order of development of the child's powers and interests. The law for presenting and treating material is the law implicit within the child's own nature. Because this is so I believe the following statements are of supreme importance as determining the spirit in which education is carried on:

1. I believe that the active side precedes the passive in the development of the child nature; that expression comes before conscious impression; that the muscular development precedes the sensory; that movements come before conscious sensations; I believe that consciousness is essentially motor or impulsive; that conscious states tend to project themselves in action.

I believe that the neglect of this principle is the cause of a large part of the waste of time and strength in school work. The child is thrown into a passive, receptive, or absorbing attitude. The conditions are such that he is not permitted to follow the law of his nature; the result is friction and waste.

I believe that ideas (intellectual and rational processes) also result from action and devolve for the sake of the better control of action. What we term reason is primarily the law of orderly or effective action. To attempt to develop the reasoning powers, the powers of judgment, without reference to the selection and arrangement of means in action, is the fundamental fallacy in our present methods of dealing with this matter. As a result we present the child with arbitrary symbols. Symbols are a necessity in mental development, but they have their place as tools for economizing effort; presented by themselves they are a mass of meaningless and arbitrary ideas imposed from without.

2. I believe that the image is the great instrument of instruction. What a child gets out of any subject presented to him is simply the images which he himself forms with regard to it.

I believe that if nine tenths of the energy at present directed towards making the child learn certain things, were spent in seeing to it that the child was forming proper images, the work of instruction would be indefinitely facilitated.

I believe that much of the time and attention now given to the preparation and presentation of lessons might be more wisely and profitably expended in training the child's power of imagery and in seeing to it that he was continually forming definite, vivid, and growing images of the various subjects with which he comes in contact in his experience.

3. I believe that interests are the signs and symptoms of growing power. I believe that they represent dawning capacities. Accordingly the constant and careful observation of interests is of the utmost importance for the educator.

I believe that these interests are to be observed as showing the state of development which the child has reached.

I believe that they prophesy the stage upon which he is about to enter.

I believe that only through the continual and sympathetic observation of childhood's interests can the adult enter into the child's life and see what it is ready for, and upon what material it could work most readily and fruitfully.

I believe that these interests are neither to be humored nor repressed. To repress interest is to substitute the adult for the child, and so to weaken intellectual curiosity and alertness, to suppress initiative, and to deaden interest. To humor the interests is to substitute the transient for the permanent. The interest is always the sign of some power below; the important thing is to discover this power. To humor the interest is to fail to penetrate below the surface and its sure result is to substitute caprice and whim for genuine interest.

4. I believe that the emotions are the reflex of actions.

I believe that to endeavor to stimulate or arouse the emotions apart from their corresponding activities, is to introduce an unhealthy and morbid state of mind.

I believe that if we can only secure right habits of action and thought, with reference to the good, the true, and the beautiful, the emotions will for the most part take care of themselves.

I believe that next to deadness and dullness, formalism and routine, our education is threatened with no greater evil than sentimentalism.

I believe that this sentimentalism is the necessary result of the attempt to divorce feeling from action.

ARTICLE V—The School and Social Progress

I believe that education is the fundamental method of social progress and reform.

I believe that all reforms which rest simply upon the enactment of law, or the threatening of certain penalties, or upon changes in mechanical or outward arrangements, are transitory and futile.

I believe that education is a regulation of the process of coming to share in the social consciousness; and that the adjustment of individual activity on the basis of this social consciousness is the only sure method of social reconstruction.

I believe that this conception has due regard for both the individualistic and socialistic ideals. It is duly individual because it recognizes the formation of a certain character as the only genuine basis of right living. It is socialistic because it recognizes that this right character is not to be formed by merely individual precept, example, or exhortation, but rather by the influence of a certain form of institutional or community life upon the individual, and that the social organism through the school, as its organ, may determine ethical results.

I believe that in the ideal school we have the reconciliation of the individualistic and the institutional ideals.

I believe that the community's duty to education is, therefore, its paramount moral duty. By law and punishment, by social agitation and discussion, society can regulate and form itself in a more or less haphazard and chance way. But through education society can formulate its own purposes, can organize its own means and resources, and thus shape itself with definiteness and economy in the direction in which it wishes to move.

I believe that when society once recognizes the possibilities in this direction, and the obligations which these possibilities impose, it is impossible to conceive of the resources of time, attention, and money which will be put at the disposal of the educator.

I believe that it is the business of every one interested in education to insist upon the school as the primary and most effective interest of social progress and reform in order that society may be awakened to realize what the school stands for, and aroused to the necessity of endowing the educator with sufficient equipment properly to perform his task.

I believe that education thus conceived marks the most perfect and intimate union of science and art conceivable in human experience.

I believe that the art of thus giving shape to human powers and adapting them to social service, is the supreme art; one calling into its service the best of artists; that no insight, sympathy, tact, executive power, is too great for such service.

I believe that with the growth of psychological service, giving added insight into individual structure and laws of growth; and with growth of social science, adding to our knowledge of the right organization of individuals, all scientific resources can be utilized for the purposes of education.

I believe that when science and art thus join hands the most commanding motive for human action will be reached; the most genuine springs of human conduct aroused and the best service that human nature is capable of guaranteed.

I believe, finally, that the teacher is engaged, not simply in the training of individuals, but in the formation of the proper social life.

I believe that every teacher should realize the dignity of his calling; that he is a social servant set apart for the maintenance of proper social order and the securing of the right social growth.

I believe that in this way the teacher always is the prophet of the true God and the usherer in of the true kingdom of God.

The School and Society*

◆

*The Laboratory School, founded by Dewey and
Mrs. Alice Chipman Dewey in 1896, was under his
direction for less than eight years. The influence of
"The Dewey School," as it came to be called, was,
however, immediate and lasting, profound and
world-wide. Dewey himself served as its principal
publicist. The three lectures on* The School and
Society *which he delivered in 1899 had as their first
purposes the refutation of cries that the School was
subversive and worse, and the raising of funds (as
the support given by the University of Chicago was
so small as to be nominal). Dewey's presentation of
principles and practice did more, however, than
justify a particular experiment. The lectures were
taken up at once as firmly establishing the worth
and practicality of the "new" idea of education as
experimental, child-centered, and directed toward
the reformation of society. Translated into a dozen
languages and later expanded, they have been the
most widely read of Dewey's writings on education
—and among the most bitterly criticized.*

I

THE SCHOOL AND SOCIAL PROGRESS

We are apt to look at the school from an individualistic
standpoint, as something between teacher and pupil, or
between teacher and parent. That which interests us
most is naturally the progress made by the individual
child of our acquaintance, his normal physical develop-

* Chicago: The University of Chicago Press, 1899, copyright 1900
by John Dewey. Chapters I, II, III.

ment, his advance in ability to read, write, and figure, his growth in the knowledge of geography and history, improvement in manners, habits of promptness, order, and industry—it is from such standards as these that we judge the work of the school. And rightly so. Yet the range of the outlook needs to be enlarged. What the best and wisest parent wants for his own child, that must the community want for all of its children. Any other ideal for our schools is narrow and unlovely; acted upon, it destroys our democracy. All that society has accomplished for itself is put, through the agency of the school, at the disposal of its future members. All its better thoughts of itself it hopes to realize through the new possibilities thus opened to its future self. Here individualism and socialism are at one. Only by being true to the full growth of all the individuals who make it up, can society by any chance be true to itself. And in the self-direction thus given, nothing counts as much as the school, for, as Horace Mann said, "Where anything is growing, one former is worth a thousand re-formers."

Whenever we have in mind the discussion of a new movement in education, it is especially necessary to take the broader, or social view. Otherwise, changes in the school institution and tradition will be looked at as the arbitrary inventions of particular teachers; at the worst transitory fads, and at the best merely improvements in certain details—and this is the plane upon which it is too customary to consider school changes. It is as rational to conceive of the locomotive or the telegraph as personal devices. The modification going on in the method and curriculum of education is as much a product of the changed social situation, and as much an effort to meet the needs of the new society that is forming, as are changes in modes of industry and commerce.

It is to this, then, that I especially ask your attention: the effort to conceive what roughly may be termed the "New Education" in the light of larger changes in society. Can we connect this "New Education" with the general march of events? If we can, it will lose its isolated character, and will cease to be an affair which proceeds only from the over-ingenious minds of pedagogues dealing with particular pupils. It will appear as part and parcel of the whole social evolution, and, in its more general features at least, as inevitable. Let us then ask after the main aspects of the social movement; and afterwards turn to the school to find what witness it gives of effort to put itself in line. And since it is quite impossible to cover the whole ground, I shall for the most part confine myself to one typical thing in the modern school movement—that which passes under the name of manual training, hoping if the relation of that to changed social conditions appears, we shall be ready to concede the point as well regarding other educational innovations.

I make no apology for not dwelling at length upon the social changes in question. Those I shall mention are writ so large that he who runs may read. The change that comes first to mind, the one that overshadows and even controls all others, is the industrial one—the application of science resulting in the great inventions that have utilized the forces of nature on a vast and inexpensive scale: the growth of a world-wide market as the object of production, of vast manufacturing centers to supply this market, of cheap and rapid means of communication and distribution between all its parts. Even as to its feebler beginnings, this change is not much more than a century old; in many of its most important aspects it falls within the short span of those now living. One can hardly believe there has been a revolution in all history so rapid, so extensive, so complete. Through it the face of the earth is making over, even as to its physical forms; political boundaries are wiped out and moved about, as if they were indeed only lines on a paper map; population is hurriedly gathered into cities from the ends of the earth; habits of living are altered with startling abruptness and thoroughness; the search for the truths of nature is infinitely stimulated and facilitated and their application to life made not only practicable, but commercially necessary. Even our moral and religious ideas and interests, the most conservative because the deepest-lying things in our nature, are profoundly affected. That this revolution should not affect education in other than formal and superficial fashion is inconceivable.

Back of the factory system lies the household and neighborhood system. Those of us who are here today need go back only one, two, or at most three generations, to find a time when the household was practically the center in which were carried on, or about which were clustered, all the typical forms of industrial occupation. The clothing worn was for the most part not only made in the house, but the members of the household were usually familiar with the shearing of the sheep, the carding and spinning of the wool, and the plying of the loom. Instead of pressing a button and flooding the house with electric light, the whole process of getting illumination was followed in its toilsome length, from the killing of the animal and the trying of fat, to the making of wicks and dipping of candles. The supply of flour, of lumber, of foods, of building materials, of household furniture, even of metal ware, of nails, hinges, hammers, etc., was in the immediate neighborhood, in shops which were constantly open to inspection and often centers of neighborhood congregation. The entire industrial process stood revealed, from the production on the farm of the raw materials, till the finished article was actually put to use. Not only this, but practically every member of the household had his own share in the work. The children, as they gained in strength and capacity, were gradually initiated into the mysteries of the several processes. It was a matter of immediate and personal concern, even to the point of actual participation.

We cannot overlook the factors of discipline and of character-building involved in this: training in habits of order and of industry, and in the idea of responsibility, of obligation to do something, to produce something, in the world. There was always something which really needed to be done, and a real necessity that each member of the household should do his own part faithfully and in coöperation with others. Personalities which became effective in action were bred and tested in the medium of action. Again, we cannot overlook the importance for educational purposes of the close and intimate acquaintance got with nature at first hand, with real things and materials, with the actual processes of their manipulation, and the knowledge of their social necessities and uses. In all this there was continual training of observation, of ingenuity, constructive imagination, of logical thought, and of the sense of reality acquired through first-hand contact with actualities. The educative forces of the domestic spinning and weaving, of the saw-mill, the grist-mill, the cooper shop, and the blacksmith forge, were continuously operative.

No number of object-lessons, got up *as* object-lessons for the sake of giving information, can afford even the shadow of a substitute for acquaintance with the plants and animals of the farm and garden, acquired through actual living among them and caring for them. No training of sense-organs in school, introduced for the sake of training, can begin to compete with the alertness and fullness of sense-life that comes through daily intimacy and interest in familiar occupations. Verbal memory can be trained in committing tasks, a certain discipline of the reasoning powers can be acquired through lessons in science and mathematics; but, after all, this is somewhat remote and shadowy compared with the training of attention and of judgment that is acquired in having to do things with a real motive behind and a real outcome ahead. At present, concentration of industry and division of labor have practically eliminated household and neighborhood occupations—at least for educational purposes. But it is useless to bemoan the departure of the good old days of children's modesty, reverence, and implicit obedience, if we expect merely by bemoaning and by exhortation to bring them back. It is radical conditions which have changed, and only an equally radical change in education suffices. We must recognize our compensations—the increase in toleration, in breadth of social judgment, the larger acquaintance with human nature, the sharpened alertness in reading signs of character and interpreting social situations, greater accuracy of adaptation to differing personalities, contact with greater commercial activities. These considerations mean much to the city-bred child of today. Yet there is a real problem: how shall we retain these advantages, and yet introduce into the school something representing the other side of life—occupations which exact personal responsibilities and which train the child with relation to the physical realities of life?

When we turn to the school, we find that one of the most striking tendencies at present is toward the introduction of so-called manual training, shop-work, and the household arts—sewing and cooking.

This has not been done "on purpose," with a full consciousness that the school must now supply that factor of training formerly taken care of in the home, but rather by instinct, by experimenting and finding that such work takes a vital hold of pupils and gives them something which was not to be got in any other way. Consciousness of its real import is still so weak that the work is often done in a half-hearted, confused, and unrelated way. The reasons assigned to justify it are painfully inadequate or sometimes even positively wrong.

If we were to cross-examine even those who are most favorably disposed to the introduction of this work into our school system, we should, I imagine, generally find the main reasons to be that such work engages the full spontaneous interest and attention of the children. It keeps them alert and active, instead of passive and receptive; it makes them more useful, more capable, and hence more inclined to be helpful at home; it prepares them to some extent for the practical duties of later life —the girls to be more efficient house managers, if not actually cooks and sempstresses; the boys (were our educational system only adequately rounded out into trade schools) for their future vocations. I do not underestimate the worth of these reasons. Of those indicated by the changed attitude of the children I shall indeed have something to say in my next talk, when speaking directly of the relationship of the school to the child. But the point of view is, upon the whole, unnecessarily narrow.

We must conceive of work in wood and metal, of weaving, sewing, and cooking, as methods of life not as distinct studies.

We must conceive of them in their social significance, as types of the processes by which society keeps itself going, as agencies for bringing home to the child some of the primal necessities of community life, and as ways in which these needs have been met by the growing insight and ingenuity of man; in short, as instrumentalities through which the school itself shall be made a genuine form of active community life, instead of a place set apart in which to learn lessons.

A society is a number of people held together because they are working along common lines, in a common spirit, and with reference to common aims. The common needs and aims demand a growing interchange of thought and growing unity of sympathetic feeling. The radical reason that the present school cannot organize itself as a natural social unit is because just this element of common and productive activity is absent. Upon the playground, in game and sport, social organization takes place spontaneously and inevitably. There is something to do, some activity to be carried on, requiring natural divisions of labor, selection of leaders and followers, mutual coöperation and emulation. In the schoolroom the motive and the cement of social organization are alike wanting. Upon the ethical side, the tragic weakness of the present school is that it endeavors to prepare future members of the social order in a medium in which the conditions of the social spirit are eminently wanting.

The difference that appears when occupations are made the articulating centers of school life is not easy to describe in words; it is a difference in motive, of spirit and atmosphere. As one enters a busy kitchen in which a group of children are actively engaged in the preparation of food, the psychological difference, the change from more or less passive and inert recipiency and restraint to one of buoyant outgoing energy, is so obvious as fairly to strike one in the face. Indeed, to those whose image of the school is rigidly set the change is sure to give a shock. But the change in the social attitude is equally marked. The mere absorption of facts and truths is so exclusively individual an affair that it tends very naturally to pass into selfishness. There is no obvious social motive for the acquirement of mere learning, there is no clear social gain in success thereat. Indeed, almost the only measure for success is a competitive one, in the bad sense of that term—a comparison of results in the recitation or in the examination to see which child has succeeded in getting ahead of others in storing up, in accumulating the maximum of information. So thoroughly is this the prevalent atmosphere that for one child to help another in his task has become a school crime. Where the school work consists in simply learning lessons, mutual assistance, instead of being the most natural form of coöperation and association, becomes a clandestine effort to relieve one's neighbor of his proper duties. Where active work is going on all this is changed. Helping others, instead of being a form of charity which impoverishes the recipient, is simply an aid in setting free the powers and furthering the impulse of the one helped. A spirit of free communication, of interchange of ideas, suggestions, results, both successes and failures of previous experiences, becomes the dominating note of the recitation. So far as emulation enters in, it is in the comparison of individuals, not with regard to the quantity of information personally absorbed, but with reference to the quality of work done—the genuine community standard of value. In an informal but all the more pervasive way, the school life organizes itself on a social basis.

Within this organization is found the principle of school discipline or order. Of course, order is simply a thing which is relative to an end. If you have the end in view of forty or fifty children learning certain set lessons, to be recited to a teacher, your discipline must be devoted to securing that result. But if the end in view is the development of a spirit of social coöperation and community life, discipline must grow out of and be relative to this. There is little order of one sort where things are in process of construction; there is a certain disorder in any busy workshop; there is not silence; persons are not engaged in maintaining certain fixed physical postures; their arms are not folded; they are not holding their books thus and so. They are doing a variety of things, and there is the confusion, the bustle, that results from activity. But out of occupation, out of doing things that are to produce results, and out of doing these in a social and coöperative way, there is born a discipline of its own kind and type. Our whole conception of school discipline changes when we get this point of view. In critical moments we all realize that the only discipline that stands by us, the only training that becomes intuition, is that got through life itself. That we learn from experience, and from books or the sayings of others *only* as they are related to experience, are not mere phrases. But the school has been so set apart, so isolated from the ordinary conditions and motives of life, that the place where children are sent for discipline is the one place in the world where it is most difficult to get experience—the mother of all discipline worth the name. It is only where a narrow and fixed image of traditional school discipline dominates, that one is in any danger of overlooking that deeper and infinitely wider discipline that comes from having a part to do in constructive work, in contributing to a result which, social in spirit, is none the less obvious and tangible in form—and hence in a form with reference to which responsibility may be exacted and accurate judgment passed.

The great thing to keep in mind, then, regarding the introduction into the school of various forms of active occupation, is that through them the entire spirit of the school is renewed. It has a chance to affiliate itself with life, to become the child's habitat, where he learns through directed living; instead of being only a place to learn lessons having an abstract and remote reference to some possible living to be done in the future. It gets a chance to be a miniature community, an embryonic society. This is the fundamental fact, and from this arise continuous and orderly sources of instruction. Under the industrial *régime* described, the child, after all, shared in the work, not for the sake of the sharing, but for the sake of the product. The educational results secured were real, yet incidental and dependent. But in the school the typical occupations followed are freed from all economic stress. The aim is not the economic value of the products, but the development of social power and insight. It is this liberation from narrow utilities, this openness to the possibilities of the human spirit that makes these practical activities in the school allies of art and centers of science and history.

The unity of all the sciences is found in geography. The significance of geography is that it presents the earth as the enduring home of the occupations of man. The world without its relationship to human activity is less than a world. Human industry and achievement, apart from their roots in the earth, are not even a sentiment, hardly a name. The earth is the final source of all man's food. It is his continual shelter and protection, the raw material of all his activities, and the home to whose humanizing and idealizing all his achievement returns. It is the great field, the great mine, the great source of the energies of heat, light, and electricity; the great scene of ocean, stream, mountain, and plain, of which all our agriculture and mining and lumbering, all our manufacturing and distributing agencies, are but the partial elements and factors. It is through occupations determined by this environment that mankind has made its historical and political progress. It is through these occupations that the intellectual and emotional interpretation of nature has been developed. It is through what we do in and with the world that we read its meaning and measure its value.

In educational terms, this means that these occupations in the school shall not be mere practical devices or modes of routine employment, the gaining of better technical skill as cooks, sempstresses, or carpenters, but active centers of scientific insight into natural materials and processes, points of departure whence children shall be led out into a realization of the historic development of man. The actual significance of this can be told better through one illustration taken from actual school work than by general discourse.

There is nothing which strikes more oddly upon the average intelligent visitor than to see boys as well as girls of ten, twelve, and thirteen years of age engaged in sewing and weaving. If we look at this from the standpoint of preparation of the boys for sewing on buttons and making patches, we get a narrow and utilitarian conception—a basis that hardly justifies giving prominence to this sort of work in the school. But if we look at it from another side, we find that this work gives the point of departure from which the child can trace and follow the progress of mankind in history, getting an insight also into the materials used and the mechanical principles involved. In connection with these occupations, the historic development of man is recapitulated. For example, the children are first given the raw material—the flax, the cotton plant, the wool as it comes from the back of the sheep (if we could take them to the place where the sheep are sheared, so much the better). Then a study is made of these materials from the standpoint of their adaptation to the uses to which they may be put. For instance, a comparison of the cotton fiber with wool fiber is made. I did not know until the children told me, that the reason for the late development of the cotton industry as compared with the woolen is, that the cotton fiber is so very difficult to free by hand from the seeds. The children in one group worked thirty minutes freeing cotton fibers from the boll and seeds, and succeeded in getting out less than one ounce. They could easily believe that one person could only gin one pound a day by hand, and could understand why their ancestors wore woolen instead of cotton clothing. Among other things discovered as affecting their relative utilities, was the shortness of the cotton fiber as compared with that of wool, the former being one-tenth of an inch in length, while that of the latter is an inch in length; also that the fibers of cotton are smooth and do not cling together, while the wool has a certain roughness which makes the fibers stick, thus assisting the spinning. The children worked this out for themselves with the actual material, aided by questions and suggestions from the teacher.

They then followed the processes necessary for working the fibers up into cloth. They re-invented the first frame for carding the wool—a couple of boards with sharp pins in them for scratching it out. They re-devised the simplest process for spinning the wool—a pierced stone or some other weight through which the wool is passed, and which as it is twirled draws out the fiber; next the top, which was spun on the floor, while the children kept the wool in their hands until it was gradually drawn out and wound upon it. Then the children are introduced to the invention next in historic order, working it out experimentally, thus seeing its necessity, and tracing its effects, not only upon that particular industry, but upon modes of social life—in this way passing in review the entire process up to the present complete loom, and all that goes with the application of science in the use of our present available powers. I need not speak of the science involved in this—the study of the fibers, of geographical features, the conditions under which raw materials are grown, the great centers of manufacture and distribution, the physics involved in the machinery of production; nor, again, of the historical side—the influence which these inventions have had upon humanity. You can concentrate the history of all mankind into the evolution of the flax, cotton, and wool fibers into clothing. I do not mean that this is the only, or the best, center. But it is true that certain very real and important avenues to the consideration of the history of the race are thus opened—that the mind is introduced to much more fundamental and controlling influences than usually appear in the political and chronological records that pass for history.

Now, what is true of this one instance of fibers used in fabrics (and, of course, I have only spoken of one or two elementary phases of that) is true in its measure of every material used in every occupation, and of the processes employed. The occupation supplies the child with a genuine motive; it gives him experience at first hand; it brings him into contact with realities. It does all this, but in addition it is liberalized throughout by translation into its historic values and scientific equivalencies. With the growth of the child's mind in power and knowledge it ceases to be a pleasant occupation merely, and becomes more and more a medium, an instrument, an organ—and is thereby transformed.

This, in turn, has its bearing upon the teaching of science. Under present conditions, all activity, to be successful, has to be directed somewhere and somehow by the scientific expert—it is a case of applied science. This connection should determine its place in education. It is not only that the occupations, the so-called manual or industrial work in the school, give the opportunity for the introduction of science which illuminates them, which makes them material, freighted with meaning, instead of being mere devices of hand and eye; but that the scientific insight thus gained becomes an indispensable instrument of free and active participation in modern social life. Plato somewhere speaks of the slave as one who in his actions does not express his own ideas, but those of some other man. It is our social problem now, even more urgent than in the time of Plato, that method, purpose, understanding, shall exist in the consciousness of the one who does the work, that his activity shall have meaning to himself.

When occupations in the school are conceived in this broad and generous way, I can only stand lost in wonder at the objections so often heard, that such occupations are out of place in the school because they are materialistic, utilitarian, or even menial in their tendency. It sometimes seems to me that those who make these objections must live in quite another world. The world in which most of us live is a world in which everyone has a calling and occupation, something to do. Some are managers and others are subordinates. But the great thing for one as for the other is that each shall have had the education which enables him to see within his daily work all there is in it of large and human significance.

How many of the employed are today mere appendages to the machines which they operate! This may be due in part to the machine itself, or to the *régime* which lays so much stress upon the products of the machine; but it is certainly due in large part to the fact that the worker has had no opportunity to develop his imagination and his sympathetic insight as to the social and scientific values found in his work. At present, the impulses which lie at the basis of the industrial system are either practically neglected or positively distorted during the school period. Until the instincts of construction and production are systematically laid hold of in the years of childhood and youth, until they are trained in social directions, enriched by historical interpretation, controlled and illuminated by scientific methods, we certainly are in no position even to locate the source of our economic evils, much less to deal with them effectively.

If we go back a few centuries, we find a practical monopoly of learning. The term *possession* of learning was, indeed, a happy one. Learning was a class matter. This was a necessary result of social conditions. There were not in existence any means by which the multitude could possibly have access to intellectual resources. These were stored up and hidden away in manuscripts. Of these there were at best only a few, and it required long and toilsome preparation to be able to do anything with them. A high-priesthood of learning, which guarded the treasury of truth and which doled it out to the masses under severe restrictions, was the inevitable expression of these conditions. But, as a direct result of the industrial revolution of which we have been speaking, this has been changed. Printing was invented; it was made commercial. Books, magazines, papers were multiplied and cheapened. As a result of the locomotive and telegraph, frequent, rapid, and cheap intercommunication by mails and electricity was called into being. Travel has been rendered easy; freedom of movement, with its accompanying exchange of ideas, indefinitely facilitated. The result has been an intellectual revolution. Learning has been put into circulation. While there still is, and probably always will be, a particular class having the special business of inquiry in hand, a distinctively learned class is henceforth out of the question. It is an anachronism. Knowledge is no longer an immobile solid; it has been liquified. It is actively moving in all the currents of society itself.

It is easy to see that this revolution, as regards the materials of knowledge, carries with it a marked change in the attitude of the individual. Stimuli of an intellectual sort pour in upon us in all kinds of ways. The merely intellectual life, the life of scholarship and of learning, thus gets a very altered value. Academic and scholastic, instead of being titles of honor, are becoming terms of reproach.

But all this means a necessary change in the attitude of the school, one of which we are as yet far from realizing the full force. Our school methods, and to a very considerable extent our curriculum, are inherited from the period when learning and command of certain symbols, affording as they did the only access to learning, were all-important. The ideals of this period are still largely in control, even where the outward methods and studies have been changed. We sometimes hear the introduction of manual training, art and science into the elementary, and even the secondary schools, deprecated on the ground that they tend toward the production of specialists—that they detract from our present scheme of generous, liberal culture. The point of this objection would be ludicrous if it were not often so effective as to make it tragic. It is our present education which is highly specialized, one-sided and narrow. It is an education dominated almost entirely by the mediæval conception of learning. It is something which appeals for the most part simply to the intellectual aspect of our natures, our desire to learn, to accumulate information, and to get control of the symbols of learning; not to our impulses and tendencies to make, to do, to create, to produce, whether in the form of utility or of art. The very fact that manual training, art and science are objected to as technical, as tending toward mere specialism, is of itself as good testimony as could be offered to the specialized aim which controls current education. Unless education had been virtually identified with the exclusively intellectual pursuits, with learning as such, all these materials and methods would be welcome, would be greeted with the utmost hospitality.

While training for the profession of learning is regarded as the type of culture, as a liberal education, that of a mechanic, a musician, a lawyer, a doctor, a farmer, a merchant, or a railroad manager is regarded as purely technical and professional. The result is that which we see about us everywhere—the division into "cultured" people and "workers," the separation of theory and practice. Hardly one per cent. of the entire school population ever attains to what we call higher education; only five per cent. to the grade of our high school; while much more than half leave on or before the completion of the fifth year of the elementary grade. The simple facts of the case are that in the great majority of human beings the distinctively intellectual interest is not dominant. They have the so-called practical impulse and disposition. In many of those in whom by nature intellectual interest is strong, social conditions prevent its adequate realization. Consequently by far the larger number of pupils leave school as soon as they have acquired the rudiments of learning, as soon as they have enough of the symbols of reading, writing, and calculating to be of practical use to them in getting a living. While our educational leaders are talking of culture, the development of personality, etc., as the end and aim of education, the great majority of those who pass under the tuition of the school regard it only as a narrowly practical tool with which to get bread and butter enough to eke out a restricted life. If we were to conceive our educational end and aim in a less exclusive way, if we were to introduce into educational processes the activities which appeal to those whose dominant interest is to do and to make, we should find the hold of the school upon its members to be more vital, more prolonged, containing more of culture.

But why should I make this labored presentation? The obvious fact is that our social life has undergone a thorough and radical change. If our education is to have any meaning for life, it must pass through an equally complete transformation. This transformation is not something to appear suddenly, to be executed in a day by conscious purpose. It is already in progress. Those modifications of our school system which often appear (even to those most actively concerned with them, to say nothing of their spectators) to be mere changes of detail, mere improvement within the school mechanism, are in reality signs and evidences of evolution. The introduction of active occupations, of nature study, of elementary science, of art, of history; the relegation of the merely symbolic and formal to a secondary position; the change in the moral school atmosphere, in the relation of pupils and teachers—of discipline; the introduction of more active, expressive, and self-directing factors—all these are not mere accidents, they are necessities of the larger social evolution. It remains but to organize all these factors, to appreciate them in their fullness of meaning, and to put the ideas and ideals involved into complete, uncompromising possession of our school system. To do this means to make each one of our schools an embryonic community life, active with types of occupations that reflect the life of the larger society, and permeated throughout with the spirit of art, history, and science. When the school introduces and trains each child of society into membership within such a little community, saturating him with the spirit of service, and providing him with the instruments of effective self-direction, we shall have the deepest and best guarantee of a larger society which is worthy, lovely, and harmonious.

II

THE SCHOOL AND THE LIFE
OF THE CHILD

Last week I tried to put before you the relationship between the school and the larger life of the community, and the necessity for certain changes in the methods and materials of school work, that it might be better adapted to present social needs.

Today I wish to look at the matter from the other side, and consider the relationship of the school to the life and development of the children in the school. As it is difficult to connect general principles with such thoroughly concrete things as little children, I have taken the liberty of introducing a good deal of illustrative matter from the work of the University Elementary School, that in some measure you may appreciate the way in which the ideas presented work themselves out in actual practice.

Some few years ago I was looking about the school supply stores in the city, trying to find desks and chairs which seemed thoroughly suitable from all points of view—artistic, hygienic, and educational—to the needs of the children. We had a good deal of difficulty in finding what we needed, and finally one dealer, more intelligent than the rest, made this remark: "I am afraid we have not what you want. You want something at which the children may work; these are all for listening." That tells the story of the traditional education. Just as the biologist can take a bone or two and reconstruct the whole animal, so, if we put before the mind's eye the ordinary schoolroom, with its rows of ugly desks placed in geometrical order, crowded together so that there shall be as little moving room as possible, desks almost all of the same size, with just space enough to hold books, pencils and paper, and add a table, some chairs, the bare walls, and possibly a few pictures, we can reconstruct the only educational activity that can possibly go on in such

a place. It is all made "for listening"—for simply studying lessons out of a book is only another kind of listening; it marks the dependency of one mind upon another.
The attitude of listening means, comparatively speaking,
passivity, absorption; that there are certain ready-made
materials which are there, which have been prepared by
the school superintendent, the board, the teacher, and
of which the child is to take in as much as possible in the
least possible time.

There is very little place in the traditional schoolroom
for the child to work. The workshop, the laboratory, the
materials, the tools with which the child may construct,
create, and actively inquire, and even the requisite space,
have been for the most part lacking. The things that
have to do with these processes have not even a definitely
recognized place in education. They are what the educational authorities who write editorials in the daily
papers generally term "fads" and "frills." A lady told
me yesterday that she had been visiting different schools
trying to find one where activity on the part of the children preceded the giving of information on the part of
the teacher, or where the children had some motive for
demanding the information. She visited, she said, twenty-
four different schools before she found her first instance.
I may add that that was not in this city.

Another thing that is suggested by these schoolrooms,
with their set desks, is that everything is arranged for
handling as large numbers of children as possible; for
dealing with children *en masse,* as an aggregate of units;
involving, again, that they be treated passively. The moment children act they individualize themselves; they
cease to be a mass, and become the intensely distinctive
beings that we are acquainted with out of school, in the
home, the family, on the playground, and in the neighborhood.

On the same basis is explicable the uniformity of
method and curriculum. If everything is on a "listening"
basis, you can have uniformity of material and method.
The ear, and the book which reflects the ear, constitute
the medium which is alike for all. There is next to no

opportunity for adjustment to varying capacities and demands. There is a certain amount—a fixed quantity— of ready-made results and accomplishments to be acquired by all children alike in a given time. It is in response to this demand that the curriculum has been developed from the elementary school up through the college. There is just so much desirable knowledge, and there are just so many needed technical accomplishments in the world. Then comes the mathematical problem of dividing this by the six, twelve, or sixteen years of school life. Now give the children every year just the proportionate fraction of the total, and by the time they have finished they will have mastered the whole. By covering so much ground during this hour or day or week or year, everything comes out with perfect evenness at the end—provided the children have not forgotten what they have previously learned. The outcome of all this is Matthew Arnold's report of the statement, proudly made to him by an educational authority in France, that so many thousands of children were studying at a given hour, say eleven o'clock, just such a lesson in geography; and in one of our own western cities this proud boast used to be repeated to successive visitors by its superintendent.

I may have exaggerated somewhat in order to make plain the typical points of the old education: its passivity of attitude, its mechanical massing of children, its uniformity of curriculum and method. It may be summed up by stating that the center of gravity is outside the child. It is in the teacher, the text-book, anywhere and everywhere you please except in the immediate instincts and activities of the child himself. On that basis there is not much to be said about the *life* of the child. A good deal might be said about the studying of the child, but the school is not the place where the child *lives*. Now the change which is coming into our education is the shifting of the center of gravity. It is a change, a revolution, not unlike that introduced by Copernicus when the astronomical center shifted from the earth to the sun. In this case the child becomes the sun about which the ap-

pliances of education revolve; he is the center about
which they are organized.

If we take an example from an ideal home, where the
parent is intelligent enough to recognize what is best for
the child, and is able to supply what is needed, we find
the child learning through the social converse and con-
stitution of the family. There are certain points of interest and value to him in the conversation carried on:
statements are made, inquiries arise, topics are discussed,
and the child continually learns. He states his experiences, his misconceptions are corrected. Again the child
participates in the household occupations, and thereby
gets habits of industry, order, and regard for the rights
and ideas of others, and the fundamental habit of subordinating his activities to the general interest of the
household. Participation in these household tasks becomes an opportunity for gaining knowledge. The ideal
home would naturally have a workshop where the child
could work out his constructive instincts. It would have
a miniature laboratory in which his inquiries could be
directed. The life of the child would extend out of doors
to the garden, surrounding fields, and forests. He would
have his excursions, his walks and talks, in which the
larger world out of doors would open to him.

Now, if we organize and generalize all of this, we have
the ideal school. There is no mystery about it, no won-
derful discovery of pedagogy or educational theory. It is
simply a question of doing systematically and in a large,
intelligent, and competent way what for various reasons
can be done in most households only in a comparatively
meager and haphazard manner. In the first place, the
ideal home has to be enlarged. The child must be
brought into contact with more grown people and with
more children in order that there may be the freest and
richest social life. Moreover, the occupations and relationships of the home environment are not specially
selected for the growth of the child; the main object is
something else, and what the child can get out of them
is incidental. Hence the need of a school. In this school
the life of the child becomes the all-controlling aim. All

the media necessary to further the growth of the child center there. Learning?—certainly, but living primarily, and learning through and in relation to this living. When we take the life of the child centered and organized in this way, we do not find that he is first of all a listening being; quite the contrary.

The statement so frequently made that education means "drawing out" is excellent, if we mean simply to contrast it with the process of pouring in. But, after all, it is difficult to connect the idea of drawing out with the ordinary doings of the child of three, four, seven, or eight years of age. He is already running over, spilling over, with activities of all kinds. He is not a purely latent being whom the adult has to approach with great caution and skill in order gradually to draw out some hidden germ of activity. The child is already intensely active, and the question of education is the question of taking hold of his activities, of giving them direction. Through direction, through organized use, they tend toward valuable results, instead of scattering or being left to merely impulsive expression.

If we keep this before us, the difficulty I find uppermost in the minds of many people regarding what is termed the new education is not so much solved as dissolved; it disappears. A question often asked is: if you begin with the child's ideas, impulses and interests, all so crude, so random and scattering, so little refined or spiritualized, how is he going to get the necessary discipline, culture and information? If there were no way open to us except to excite and indulge these impulses of the child, the question might well be asked. We should either have to ignore and repress the activities, or else to humor them. But if we have organization of equipment and of materials, there is another path open to us. We can direct the child's activities, giving them exercise along certain lines, and can thus lead up to the goal which logically stands at the end of the paths followed.

"If wishes were horses, beggars would ride." Since they are not, since really to satisfy an impulse or interest means to work it out, and working it out involves running up against obstacles, becoming acquainted with materials, exercising ingenuity, patience, persistence, alertness, it of necessity involves discipline—ordering of power—and supplies knowledge. Take the example of the little child who wants to make a box. If he stops short with the imagination or wish, he certainly will not get discipline. But when he attempts to realize his impulse, it is a question of making his idea definite, making it into a plan, of taking the right kind of wood, measuring the parts needed, giving them the necessary proportions, etc. There is involved the preparation of materials, the sawing, planing, the sand-papering, making all the edges and corners to fit. Knowledge of tools and processes is inevitable. If the child realizes his instinct and makes the box, there is plenty of opportunity to gain discipline and perseverance, to exercise effort in overcoming obstacles, and to attain as well a great deal of information.

So undoubtedly the little child who thinks he would like to cook has little idea of what it means or costs, or what it requires. It is simply a desire to "mess around," perhaps to imitate the activities of older people. And it is doubtless possible to let ourselves down to that level and simply humor that interest. But here, too, if the impulse is exercised, utilized, it runs up against the actual world of hard conditions, to which it must accommodate itself; and there again come in the factors of discipline and knowledge. One of the children became impatient recently, at having to work things out by a long method of experimentation, and said: "Why do we bother with this? Let's follow a recipe in a cook-book." The teacher asked the children where the recipe came from, and the conversation showed that if they simply followed this they would not understand the reasons for what they were doing. They were then quite willing to go on with the experimental work. To follow that work will, indeed, give an illustration of just the point in question. Their occupation happened that day to be the cooking of eggs, as making a transition from the cooking of vegetables to that of meats. In order to get a basis of comparison they

first summarized the constituent food elements in the
vegetables and made a preliminary comparison with
those found in meat. Thus they found that the woody
fiber or cellulose in vegetables corresponded to the con-
nective tissue in meat, giving the element of form and
structure. They found that starch and starchy products
were characteristic of the vegetables, that mineral salts
were found in both alike, and that there was fat in both
—a small quantity in vegetable food and a large amount
in animal. They were prepared then to take up the study
of albumen as the characteristic feature of animal food,
corresponding to starch in the vegetables, and were ready
to consider the conditions requisite for the proper treatment of albumen—the eggs serving as the material of
experiment.

They experimented first by taking water at various
temperatures, finding out when it was scalding, simmer-
ing, and boiling hot, and ascertained the effect of the
various degrees of temperature on the white of the egg.
That worked out, they were prepared, not simply to cook
eggs, but to understand the principle involved in the
cooking of eggs. I do not wish to lose sight of the universal in the particular incident. For the child simply to
desire to cook an egg, and accordingly drop it in water
for three minutes, and take it out when he is told, is not
educative. But for the child to realize his own impulse
by recognizing the facts, materials and conditions involved, and then to regulate his impulse through that
recognition, is educative. This is the difference, upon
which I wish to insist, between exciting or indulging an
interest and realizing it through its direction.

Another instinct of the child is the use of pencil and
paper. All children like to express themselves through
the medium of form and color. If you simply indulge
this interest by letting the child go on indefinitely, there
is no growth that is more than accidental. But let the
child first express his impulse, and then through criticism, question, and suggestion bring him to consciousness
of what he has done, and what he needs to do, and the
result is quite different. Here, for example, is the work

of a seven-year-old child. It is not average work, it is the best work done among the little children, but it illustrates the particular principle of which I have been speaking. They had been talking about the primitive conditions of social life when people lived in caves. The child's idea of that found expression in this way: the cave is neatly set up on the hill side in an impossible way. You see the conventional tree of childhood; a vertical line with horizontal branches on each side. If the child had been allowed to go on repeating this sort of thing day by day, he would be indulging his instinct rather than exercising it. But the child was now asked to look closely at trees, to compare those seen with the one drawn, to examine more closely and consciously into the conditions of his work. Then he drew trees from observation.

Finally he drew again from combined observation, memory, and imagination. He made again a free illustration, expressing his own imaginative thought, but controlled by detailed study of actual trees. The result was a scene representing a bit of forest; so far as it goes, it seems to me to have as much poetic feeling as the work of an adult, while at the same time its trees are, in their proportions possible ones, not mere symbols.

If we roughly classify the impulses which are available in the school, we may group them under four heads. There is the social instinct of the children as shown in conversation, personal intercourse, and communication. We all know how self-centered the little child is at the age of four or five. If any new subject is brought up, if he says anything at all, it is: "I have seen that;" or "My papa or mamma told me about that." His horizon is not large; an experience must come immediately home to him, if he is to be sufficiently interested to relate it to others and seek theirs in return. And yet the egoistic and limited interest of little children is in this manner capable of infinite expansion. The language instinct is the simplest form of the social expression of the child. Hence it is a great, perhaps the greatest of all educational resources.

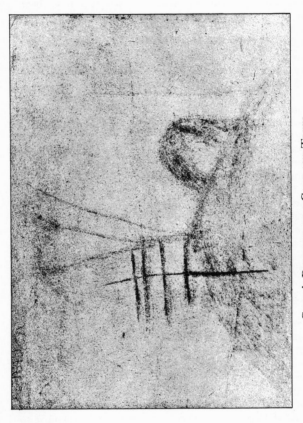

CHILD'S DRAWING OF A CAVE AND TREES

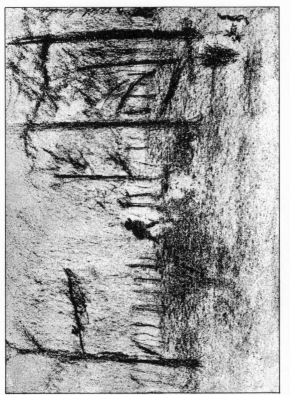

CHILD'S DRAWING OF A FOREST

59

Then there is the instinct of making—the constructive impulse. The child's impulse to do finds expression first in play, in movement, gesture, and make-believe, becomes more definite, and seeks outlet in shaping materials into tangible forms and permanent embodiment. The child has not much instinct for abstract inquiry. The instinct of investigation seems to grow out of the combination of the constructive impulse with the conversational. There is no distinction between experimental science for little children and the work done in the carpenter shop. Such work as they can do in physics or chemistry is not for the purpose of making technical generalizations or even arriving at abstract truths. Children simply like to do things, and watch to see what will happen. But this can be taken advantage of, can be directed into ways where it gives results of value, as well as be allowed to go on at random.

And so the expressive impulse of the children, the art instinct, grows also out of the communicating and constructive instincts. It is their refinement and full manifestation. Make the construction adequate, make it full, free, and flexible, give it a social motive, something to tell, and you have a work of art. Take one illustration of this in connection with the textile work—sewing and weaving. The children make a primitive loom in the shop; here the constructive instinct was appealed to. Then they wished to do something with this loom, to make something. It was the type of the Indian loom, and they were shown blankets woven by the Indians. Each child made a design kindred in idea to those of the Navajo blankets, and the one which seemed best adapted to the work in hand was selected. The technical resources were limited, but the coloring and form were worked out by the children. The example shown was made by the twelve-year-old children. Examination shows that it took patience, thoroughness, and perseverance to do the work. It involved not merely discipline and information of both a historical sort and the elements of technical design, but also something of the spirit of art in adequately conveying an idea.

One more instance of the connection of the art side
with the constructive side. The children had been studying primitive spinning and carding, when one of them,
twelve years of age, made a picture of one of the older
children spinning. Here is another piece of work which
is not quite average; it is better than the average. It
is an illustration of two hands and the drawing out of
the wool to get it ready for spinning. This was done by
a child eleven years of age. But, upon the whole, with
the younger children especially, the art impulse is connected mainly with the social instinct—the desire to tell,
to represent.

Now, keeping in mind these fourfold interests—the
interest in conversation or communication; in inquiry,
or finding out things; in making things, or construction;
and in artistic expression—we may say they are the natural resources, the uninvested capital, upon the exercise
of which depends the active growth of the child. I wish
to give one or two illustrations, the first from the work
of children seven years of age. It illustrates in a way the
dominant desire of the children to talk, particularly
about folks and of things in relation to folks. If you observe little children, you will find they are interested in
the world of things mainly in its connection with people,
as a background and medium of human concerns. Many
anthropologists have told us there are certain identities
in the child interests with those of primitive life. There
is a sort of natural recurrence of the child mind to the
typical activities of primitive peoples; witness the hut
which the boy likes to build in the yard, playing hunt,
with bows, arrows, spears, and so on. Again the question
comes: What are we to do with this interest—are we to
ignore it, or just excite and draw it out? Or shall we
get hold of it and direct it to something ahead, something better? Some of the work that has been planned for
our seven-year-old children has the latter end in view—
to utilize this interest so that it shall become a means of
seeing the progress of the human race. The children
begin by imagining present conditions taken away until
they are in contact with nature at first hand. That takes

CHILD'S DRAWING OF A GIRL SPINNING

CHILD'S DRAWING OF HANDS SPINNING

them back to the hunting people, to a people living in
caves or trees and getting a precarious subsistence by
hunting and fishing. They imagine as far as possible the
various natural physical conditions adapted to that sort
of life; say, a hilly, woody slope, near mountains and
a river where fish would be abundant. Then they go on
in imagination through the hunting to the semi-agricul-
tural stage, and through the nomadic to the settled agricultural stage. The point I wish to make is that there
is abundant opportunity thus given for actual study, for
inquiry which results in gaining information. So, while
the instinct primarily appeals to the social side, the interest of the child in people and their doings is carried
on into the larger world of reality. For example, the
children had some idea of primitive weapons, of the
stone arrowhead, etc. That provided occasion for the
testing of materials as regards their friability, their shape,
texture, etc., resulting in a lesson in mineralogy, as they
examined the different stones to find which was best
suited to the purpose. The discussion of the iron age
supplied a demand for the construction of a smelting
oven made out of clay, and of considerable size. As the
children did not get their drafts right at first, the mouth
of the furnace not being in proper relation to the vent,
as to size and position, instruction in the principles of
combustion, the nature of drafts and of fuel, was required. Yet the instruction was not given ready-made;
it was first needed, and then arrived at experimentally.
Then the children took some material, such as copper,
and went through a series of experiments, fusing it, working it into objects; and the same experiments were made
with lead and other metals. This work has been also a
continuous course in geography, since the children have
had to imagine and work out the various physical conditions necessary to the different forms of social life implied. What would be the physical conditions appropriate to pastoral life? to the beginning of agriculture? to
fishing? What would be the natural method of exchange
between these peoples? Having worked out such points
in conversation, they have afterward represented them in

maps and sand-molding. Thus they have gained ideas of the various forms of the configuration of the earth, and at the same time have seen them in their relation to human activity, so that they are not simply external facts, but are fused and welded with social conceptions regarding the life and progress of humanity. The result, to my mind, justifies completely the conviction that children, in a year of such work (of five hours a week altogether), get indefinitely more acquaintance with facts of science, geography, and anthropology than they get where information is the professed end and object, where they are simply set to learning facts in fixed lessons. As to discipline, they get more training of attention, more power of interpretation, of drawing inferences, of acute observation and continuous reflection, than if they were put to working out arbitrary problems simply for the sake of discipline.

I should like at this point to refer to the recitation. We all know what it has been—a placer* where the child shows off to the teacher and the other children the amount of information he has succeeded in assimilating from the text-book. From this other standpoint, the recitation becomes preëminently a social meeting place; it is to the school what the spontaneous conversation is at home, excepting that it is more organized, following definite lines. The recitation becomes the social clearing-house, where experiences and ideas are exchanged and subjected to criticism, where misconceptions are corrected, and new lines of thought and inquiry are set up.

This change of the recitation from an examination of knowledge already acquired to the free play of the children's communicative instinct, affects and modifies all the language work of the school. Under the old *régime* it was unquestionably a most serious problem to give the children a full and free use of language. The reason was obvious. The natural motive for language was seldom offered. In the pedagogical text-books language is defined as the medium of expressing thought. It becomes that,

* Place. *M.S.D.*

more or less, to adults with trained minds, but it hardly needs to be said that language is primarily a social thing, a means by which we give our experiences to others and get theirs again in return. When it is taken from its natural basis, it is no wonder that it becomes a complex and difficult problem to teach language. Think of the absurdity of having to teach language as a thing by itself. If there is anything the child will do before he goes to school, it is to talk of the things that interest him. But when there are not vital interests appealed to in the school, when language is used simply for the repetition of lessons, it is not surprising that one of the chief difficulties of school work has come to be instruction in the mother-tongue. Since the language taught is unnatural, not growing out of the real desire to communicate vital impressions and convictions, the freedom of children in its use gradually disappears, until finally the high-school teacher has to invent all kinds of devices to assist in getting any spontaneous and full use of speech. Moreover, when the language instinct is appealed to in a social way, there is a continual contact with reality. The result is that the child always has something in his mind to talk about, he has something to say; he has a thought to express, and a thought is not a thought unless it is one's own. On the traditional method, the child must say something that he has merely learned. There is all the difference in the world between having something to say and having to say something. The child who has a variety of materials and facts wants to talk about them, and his language becomes more refined and full, because it is controlled and informed by realities. Reading and writing, as well as the oral use of language, may be taught on this basis. It can be done in a *related* way, as the outgrowth of the child's social desire to recount his experiences and get in return the experiences of others, directed always through contact with the facts and forces which determine the truth communicated.

I shall not have time to speak of the work of the older children, where the original crude instincts of construction and communication have been developed into something like scientifically directed inquiry, but I will give an illustration of the use of language following upon this experimental work. The work was on the basis of a simple experiment of the commonest sort, gradually leading the children out into geological and geographical study. The sentences that I am going to read seem to me poetic as well as "scientific." "A long time ago when the earth was new, when it was lava, there was no water on the earth, and there was steam all round the earth up in the air, as there were many gases in the air. One of them was carbon dioxide. The steam became clouds, because the earth began to cool off, and after a while it began to rain, and the water came down and dissolved the carbon dioxide from the air." There is a good deal more science in that than probably would be apparent at the outset. It represents some three months of work on the part of the child. The children kept daily and weekly records, but this is part of the summing up of the quarter's work. I call this language poetic, because the child has a clear image and has a personal feeling for the realities imaged. I extract sentences from two other records to illustrate further the vivid use of language when there is a vivid experience back of it. "When the earth was cold enough to condense, the water, with the help of carbon dioxide, *pulls* the calcium out of the rocks into a large body of water where the little animals could get it." The other reads as follows: "When the earth cooled, calcium was in the rocks. Then the carbon dioxide and water united and formed a solution, and, as it ran, it *tore* out the calcium and carried it on to the sea, where there were little animals who took it out of solution." The use of such words as "pulled" and "tore" in connection with the process of chemical combination evidences a personal realization which compels its own appropriate expression.

If I had not taken so much time in my other illustrations, I should like to show how, beginning with very simple material things, the children were led on to larger fields of investigation, and to the intellectual discipline that is the accompaniment of such research. I will sim-

ply mention the experiment in which the work began.
It consisted in making precipitated chalk, used for polish-
ing metals. The children, with simple apparatus—a tum-
bler, lime water, and a glass tube—precipitated the calcium carbonate out of the water; and from this beginning went on to a study of the processes by which rocks
of various sorts, igneous, sedimentary, etc., had been
formed on the surface of the earth and the places they
occupy; then to points in the geography of the United
States, Hawaii, and Puerto Rico; to the effects of these
various bodies of rocks, in their various configurations,
upon the human occupations; so that this geological record finally rounded itself out into the life of man at the
present time. The children saw and felt the connection
between these geologic processes taking place ages and
ages ago, and the physical conditions determining the
industrial occupations of today.

Of all the possibilities involved in the subject, "The
School and the Life of the Child," I have selected but
one, because I have found that that one gives people more
difficulty, is more of a stumbling-block, than any other.
One may be ready to admit that it would be most desirable for the school to be a place in which the child
should really live, and get a life-experience in which he
should delight and find meaning for its own sake. But
then we hear this inquiry: how, upon this basis, shall the
child get the needed information; how shall he undergo
the required discipline? Yes, it has come to this, that
with many, if not most, people the normal processes of
life appear to be incompatible with getting information
and discipline. So I have tried to indicate, in a highly
general and inadequate way (for only the school itself, in
its daily operation, could give a detailed and worthy representation), how the problem works itself out—how it is
possible to lay hold upon the rudimentary instincts of
human nature, and, by supplying a proper medium, so
control their expression as not only to facilitate and en-
rich the growth of the individual child, but also to
supply the results, and far more, of technical information
and discipline that have been the ideals of education in
the past.

But although I have selected this especial way of approach (as a concession to the question almost universally raised), I am not willing to leave the matter in this more or less negative and explanatory condition. Life is the great thing after all; the life of the child at its time and in its measure, no less than the life of the adult. Strange would it be, indeed, if intelligent and serious attention to what the child *now* needs and is capable of in the way of a rich, valuable, and expanded life should somehow conflict with the needs and possibilities of later, adult life. "Let us live with our children," certainly means, first of all, that our children shall live—not that they shall be hampered and stunted by being forced into all kinds of conditions, the most remote consideration of which is relevancy to the present life of the child. If we seek the kingdom of heaven, educationally, all other things shall be added unto us—which, being interpreted, is that if we identify ourselves with the real instincts and needs of childhood, and ask only after its fullest assertion and growth, the discipline and information and culture of adult life shall all come in their due season.

Speaking of culture reminds me that in a way I have been speaking only of the outside of the child's activity —only of the outward expression of his impulses toward saying, making, finding out, and creating. The real child, it hardly need be said, lives in the world of imaginative values, and ideas which find only imperfect outward embodiment. We hear much nowadays about the cultivation of the child's "imagination." Then we undo much of our own talk and work by a belief that the imagination is some special part of the child, that finds its satisfaction in some one particular direction—generally speaking, that of the unreal and make-believe, of the myth and made-up story. Why are we so hard of heart and so slow to believe? The imagination is the medium in which the child lives. To him there is everywhere and in everything that occupies his mind and activity at all, a surplusage of value and significance. The question of the relation of the school to the child's life is at bottom simply this: shall we ignore this native setting and tendency, dealing not with the living child at all, but with the dead image we have erected, or shall we give it play and satisfaction? If we once believe in life and the life of the child, then will all the occupations and uses spoken of, then will all history and science, become instruments of appeal and materials of culture to his imagination, and through that to the richness and the orderliness of his life. Where we now see only the outward doing and the outward product, there, behind all visible results, is the re-adjustment of mental attitude, the enlarged and sympathetic vision, the sense of growing power, and the willing ability to identify both insight and capacity with the interests of the world and man. Unless culture be a superficial polish, a veneering of mahogany over common wood, it surely is this—the growth of the imagination in flexibility, in scope, and in sympathy, till the life which the individual lives is informed with the life of nature and of society. When nature and society can live in the schoolroom, when the forms and tools of learning are subordinated to the substance of experience, then shall there be an opportunity for this identification, and culture shall be the democratic password.

III

WASTE IN EDUCATION

The subject announced for today was "Waste in Education." I should like first to state briefly its relation to the two preceding lectures. The first dealt with the school in its social aspects, and the necessary re-adjustments that have to be made to render it effective in present social conditions. The second dealt with the school in relation to the growth of individual children. Now the third deals with the school as itself an institution, both in relation to society and to its own members—the children. It deals with the question of organization, because all waste is the result of the lack of it, the motive lying behind organization being promotion of economy and efficiency. This question is not one of the waste of money or the waste of things. These matters count; but the primary waste is that of human life, the life of the children while they are at school, and afterward because of inadequate and perverted preparation.

So, when we speak of organization, we are not to think simply of the externals; of that which goes by the name "school system"—the school board, the superintendent, and the building, the engaging and promotion of teachers, etc. These things enter in, but the fundamental organization is that of the school itself as a community of individuals, in its relations to other forms of social life. All waste is due to isolation. Organization is nothing but getting things into connection with one another, so that they work easily, flexibly, and fully. Therefore in speaking of this question of waste in education, I desire to call your attention to the isolation of the various parts of the school system, to the lack of unity in the aims of education, to the lack of coherence in its studies and methods.

I have made a chart (I) which, while I speak of the isolations of the school system itself, may perhaps appeal to the eye and save a little time in verbal explanations. A paradoxical friend of mine says there is nothing so obscure as an illustration, and it is quite possible that my attempt to illustrate my point will simply prove the truth of his statement.

The blocks represent the various elements in the school system, and are intended to indicate roughly the length of time given to each division, and also the overlapping, both in time and subjects studied, of the individual parts of the system. With each block is given the historical conditions in which it arose and its ruling ideal.

The school system, upon the whole, has grown from the top down. During the middle ages it was essentially a cluster of professional schools—especially law and theology. Our present university comes down to us from the middle ages. I will not say that at present it is a mediæval institution, but it had its roots in the middle

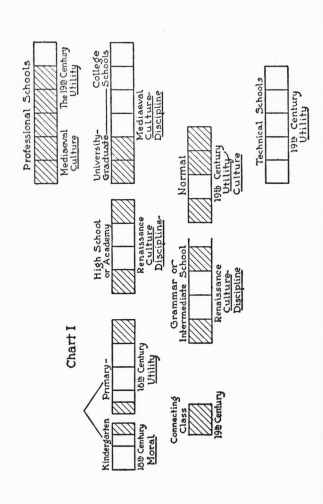

Chart I

ages, and it has not outlived all mediæval traditions regarding learning.

The kindergarten, rising with the present century, was a union of the nursery and of the philosophy of Schelling; a wedding of the plays and games which the mother carried on with her children, to Schelling's highly romantic and symbolic philosophy. The elements that came from the actual study of child life—the continuation of the nursery—have remained a life-bringing force in all education; the Schellingesque factors made an obstruction between it and the rest of the school system, brought about isolations.

The line drawn over the top indicates that there is a certain interaction between the kindergarten and the primary school; for, so far as the primary school remained in spirit foreign to the natural interests of child life, it was isolated from the kindergarten, so that it is a problem, at present, to introduce kindergarten methods into the primary school; the problem of the so-called connecting class. The difficulty is that the two are not one from the start. To get a connection the teacher has had to climb over the wall instead of entering in at the gate.

On the side of aims, the ideal of the kindergarten was the moral development of the children, rather than instruction or discipline; an ideal sometimes emphasized to the point of sentimentality. The primary school grew practically out of the popular movement of the sixteenth century, when along with the invention of printing and the growth of commerce, it became a business necessity to know how to read, write, and figure. The aim was distinctly a practical one; it was utility; getting command of these tools, the symbols of learning, not for the sake of learning, but because they gave access to careers in life otherwise closed.

The division next to the primary school is the grammar school. The term is not much used in the West, but is common in the eastern states. It goes back to the time of the revival of learning—a little earlier perhaps than the conditions out of which the primary school originated, and, even when contemporaneous, having a different ideal. It had to do with the study of language in the higher sense; because, at the time of the Renaissance, Latin and Greek connected people with the culture of the past, with the Roman and Greek world. The classic languages were the only means of escape from the limitations of the middle ages. Thus there sprang up the prototype of the grammar school, more liberal than the university (so largely professional in character), for the purpose of putting into the hands of the people the key to the old learning, that men might see a world with a larger horizon. The object was primarily culture, secondarily discipline. It represented much more than the present grammar school. It was the liberal element in the college, which, extending downward, grew into the academy and the high school. Thus the secondary school is still in part just a lower college (having an even higher curriculum than the college of a few centuries ago) or a preparatory department to a college, and in part a rounding up of the utilities of the elementary school.

There appear then two products of the nineteenth century, the technical and normal schools. The schools of technology, engineering, etc., are, of course, mainly the development of nineteenth-century business conditions, as the primary school was the development of business conditions of the sixteenth century. The normal school arose because of the necessity for training teachers, with the idea partly of professional drill, and partly that of culture.

Without going into more detail, we have some eight different parts of the school system as represented on the chart, all of which arose historically at different times, having different ideals in view, and consequently different methods. I do not wish to suggest that all of the isolation, all of the separation, that has existed in the past between the different parts of the school system still persists. One must, however, recognize that they have never yet been welded into one complete whole. The great problem in education on the administrative side is how to unite these different parts.

Consider the training schools for teachers—the normal schools. These occupy at present a somewhat anomalous position, intermediate between the high school and the college, requiring the high-school preparation, and covering a certain amount of college work. They are isolated from the higher subject-matter of scholarship, since, upon the whole, their object has been to train persons *how* to teach, rather than *what* to teach; while, if we go to the college, we find the other half of this isolation—learning *what* to teach, with almost a contempt for methods of teaching. The college is shut off from contact with children and youth. Its members, to a great extent, away from home and forgetting their own childhood, become eventually teachers with a large amount of subject-matter at command, and little knowledge of how this is related to the minds of those to whom it is to be taught. In this division between what to teach and how to teach, each side suffers from the separation.

It is interesting to follow out the inter-relation between primary, grammar, and high schools. The elementary school has crowded up and taken many subjects previously studied in the old New England grammar school. The high school has pushed its subjects down. Latin and algebra have been put in the upper grades, so that the seventh and eighth grades are, after all, about all that is left of the old grammar school. They are a sort of amorphous composite, being partly a place where children go on learning what they already have learned (to read, write, and figure), and partly a place of preparation for the high school. The name in some parts of New England for these upper grades was "Intermediate School." The term was a happy one; the work was simply intermediate between something that had been and something that was going to be, having no special meaning on its own account.

Just as the parts are separated, so do the ideals differ—moral development, practical utility, general culture, discipline, and professional training. These aims are each especially represented in some distinct part of the system of education; and with the growing interaction of the parts, each is supposed to afford a certain amount of culture, discipline, and utility. But the lack of fundamental unity is witnessed in the fact that one study is still considered good for discipline, and another for culture; some parts of arithmetic, for example, for discipline and others for use, literature for culture, grammar for discipline, geography partly for utility, partly for culture; and so on. The unity of education is dissipated, and the studies become centrifugal; so much of this study to secure this end, so much of that to secure another, until the whole becomes a sheer compromise and patchwork between contending aims and disparate studies. The great problem in education on the administrative side is to secure the unity of the whole, in the place of a sequence of more or less unrelated and overlapping parts and thus to reduce the waste arising from friction, reduplication and transitions that are not properly bridged.

In this second symbolic diagram (II) I wish to suggest that really the only way to unite the parts of the system is to unite each to life. We can get only an artificial unity so long as we confine our gaze to the school system itself. We must look at it as part of the larger whole of social life. This block (A) in the center represents the school system as a whole. (1) At one side we have the home, and the two arrows represent the free interplay of influences, materials, and ideas between the home life and that of the school. (2) Below we have the relation to the natural environment, the great field of geography in the widest sense. The school building has about it a natural environment. It ought to be in a garden, and the children from the garden would be led on to surrounding fields, and then into the wider country, with all its facts and forces. (3) Above is represented business life, and the necessity for free play between the school and the needs and forces of industry. (4) On the other side is the university proper, with its various phases, its laboratories, its resources in the way of libraries, museums, and professional schools.

From the standpoint of the child, the great waste in the school comes from his inability to utilize the experi-

Chart II

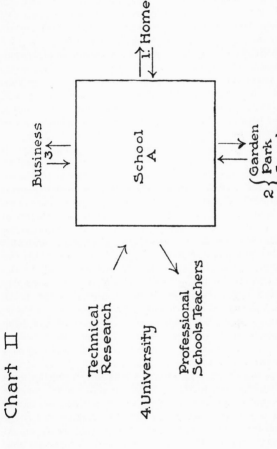

ences he gets outside the school in any complete and free way within the school itself; while, on the other hand, he is unable to apply in daily life what he is learning at school. That is the isolation of the school—its isolation from life. When the child gets into the schoolroom he has to put out of his mind a large part of the ideas, interests, and activities that predominate in his home and neighborhood. So the school, being unable to utilize this everyday experience, sets painfully to work, on another tack and by a variety of means, to arouse in the child an interest in school studies. While I was visiting in the city of Moline a few years ago, the superintendent told me that they found many children every year, who were surprised to learn that the Mississippi river in the text-book had anything to do with the stream of water flowing past their homes. The geography being simply a matter of the schoolroom, it is more or less of an awakening to many children to find that the whole thing is nothing but a more formal and definite statement of the facts which they see, feel, and touch every day. When we think that we all live on the earth, that we live in an atmosphere, that our lives are touched at every point by the influences of the soil, flora, and fauna, by considerations of light and heat, and then think of what the school study of geography has been, we have a typical idea of the gap existing between the everyday experiences of the child, and the isolated material supplied in such large measure in the school. This is but an instance, and one upon which most of us may reflect long before we take the present artificiality of the school as other than a matter of course or necessity.

Though there should be organic connection between the school and business life, it is not meant that the school is to prepare the child for any particular business, but that there should be a natural connection of the everyday life of the child with the business environment about him, and that it is the affair of the school to clarify and liberalize this connection, to bring it to consciousness, not by introducing special studies, like commercial geography and arithmetic, but by keeping alive the ordinary bonds of relation. The subject of compound-business-partnership is probably not in many of the arithmetics nowadays, though it was there not a generation ago, for the makers of text-books said that if they left out anything they could not sell their books. This compound-business-partnership originated as far back as the sixteenth century. The joint-stock company had not been invented, and as large commerce with the Indies and Americas grew up, it was necessary to have an accumulation of capital with which to handle it. One man said, "I will put in this amount of money for six months," and another, "So much for two years," and so on. Thus by joining together they got money enough to float their commercial enterprises. Naturally, then, "compound partnership" was taught in the schools. The joint-stock company was invented; compound partnership disappeared, but the problems relating to it stayed in the arithmetics for two hundred years. They were kept after they had ceased to have practical utility, for the sake of mental discipline—they were "such hard problems, you know." A great deal of what is now in the arithmetics under the head of percentage is of the same nature. Children of twelve and thirteen years of age go through gain and loss calculations, and various forms of bank discount so complicated that the bankers long ago dispensed with them. And when it is pointed out that business is not done this way, we hear again of "mental discipline." And yet there are plenty of real connections between the experience of children and business conditions which need to be utilized and illuminated. The child should study his commercial arithmetic and geography, not as isolated things by themselves, but in their reference to his social environment. The youth needs to become acquainted with the bank as a factor in modern life, with what it does, and how it does it; and then relevant arithmetical processes would have some meaning—quite in contradistinction to the time-absorbing and mind-killing examples in percentage, partial payments, etc., found in all our arithmetics.

The connection with the university, as indicated in

this chart, I need not dwell upon. I simply wish to indicate that there ought to be a free interaction between
all the parts of the school system. There is much of utter
triviality of subject-matter in elementary and secondary
education. When we investigate it, we find that it is full
of facts taught that are not facts, which have to be un-
learned later on. Now, this happens because the "lower"
parts of our system are not in vital connection with the
"higher." The university or college, in its idea, is a place
of research, where investigation is going on, a place of
libraries and museums, where the best resources of the
past are gathered, maintained and organized. It is, however, as true in the school as in the university that the
spirit of inquiry can be got only through and with the
attitude of inquiry. The pupil must learn what has meaning, what enlarges his horizon, instead of mere trivialities.
He must become acquainted with truths, instead of
things that were regarded as such fifty years ago, or that
are taken as interesting by the misunderstanding of a
partially educated teacher. It is difficult to see how these
ends can be reached except as the most advanced part
of the educational system is in complete interaction with
the most rudimentary.

The next chart (III) is an enlargement of the second.
The school building has swelled out, so to speak, the surrounding environment remaining the same, the home,
the garden and country, the relation to business life and
the university. The object is to show what the school
must become to get out of its isolation and secure the
organic connection with social life of which we have
been speaking. It is not our architect's plan for the
school building that we hope to have; but it is a diagram-
matic representation of the idea which we want embodied
in the school building. On the lower side you see the
dining-room and the kitchen, at the top the wood and
metal shops, and the textile room for sewing and weaving. The center represents the manner in which all come
together in the library; that is to say, in a collection of
the intellectual resources of all kinds that throw light
upon the practical work, that give it meaning and liberal

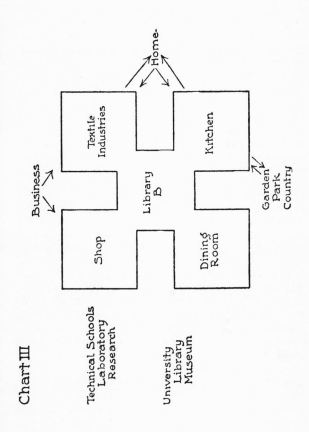

Chart III

value. If the four corners represent practice, the interior
represents the theory of the practical activities. In other
words, the object of these forms of practice in the school
is not found chiefly in themselves, or in the technical
skill of cooks, seamstresses, carpenters and masons, but
in their connection, on the social side, with the life without; while on the individual side they respond to the
child's need of action, of expression, of desire to do something, to be constructive and creative, instead of simply
passive and conforming. Their great significance is that
they keep the balance between the social and individual
sides—the chart symbolizing particularly the connection
with the social. Here on one side is the home. How
naturally the lines of connection play back and forth
between the home and the kitchen and the textile room
of the school! The child can carry over what he learns
in the home and utilize it in the school; and the things
learned in the school he applies at home. These are the
two great things in breaking down isolation, in getting
connection—to have the child come to school with all
the experience he has got outside the school, and to leave
it with something to be immediately used in his everyday life. The child comes to the traditional school with
a healthy body and a more or less unwilling mind,
though, in fact, he does not bring both his body and
mind with him; he has to leave his mind behind, because
there is no way to use it in the school. If he had a purely
abstract mind, he could bring it to school with him, but
his is a concrete one, interested in concrete things, and
unless these things get over into school life, he cannot
take his mind with him. What we want is to have the
child come to school with a whole mind and a whole
body, and leave school with a fuller mind and an even
healthier body. And speaking of the body suggests that,
while there is no gymnasium in these diagrams, the active
life carried on in its four corners brings with it constant
physical exercise, while our gymnasium proper will deal
with the particular weaknesses of children and their
correction, and will attempt more consciously to build

up the thoroughly sound body as the abode of the sound mind.

That the dining-room and kitchen connect with the country and its processes and products it is hardly necessary to say. Cooking may be so taught that it has no connection with country life, and with the sciences that find their unity in geography. Perhaps it generally has been taught without these connections being really made. But all the materials that come into the kitchen have their origin in the country; they come from the soil, are nurtured through the influences of light and water, and represent a great variety of local environments. Through this connection, extending from the garden into the larger world, the child has his most natural introduction to the study of the sciences. Where did these things grow? What was necessary to their growth? What their relation to the soil? What the effect of different climatic conditions? and so on. We all know what the old-fashioned botany was: partly collecting flowers that were pretty, pressing and mounting them; partly pulling these flowers to pieces and giving technical names to the different parts, finding all the different leaves, naming all their different shapes and forms. It was a study of plants without any reference to the soil, to the country, or to growth. In contrast, a real study of plants takes them in their natural environment and in their uses as well, not simply as food, but in all their adaptations to the social life of man. Cooking becomes as well a most natural introduction to the study of chemistry, giving the child here also something which he can at once bring to bear upon his daily experience. I once heard a very intelligent woman say that she could not understand how science could be taught to little children, because she did not see how they could understand atoms and molecules. In other words, since she did not see how highly abstract facts could be presented to the child independently of daily experience, she could not understand how science could be taught at all. Before we smile at this remark, we need to ask ourselves if she is alone in her assumption, or whether it simply formulates almost all of our school practice.

The same relations with the outside world are found in the carpentry and the textile shops. They connect with the country, as the source of their materials, with physics, as the science of applying energy, with commerce and distribution, with art in the development of architecture and decoration. They have also an intimate connection with the university on the side of its technological and engineering schools; with the laboratory, and its scientific methods and results.

To go back to the square which is marked the library (Chart III, A*): if you imagine rooms half in the four corners and half in the library, you will get the idea of the recitation room. That is the place where the children bring the experiences, the problems, the questions, the particular facts which they have found, and discuss them so that new light may be thrown upon them, particularly new light from the experience of others, the accumulated wisdom of the world—symbolized in the library. Here is the organic relation of theory and practice; the child not simply doing things, but getting also the *idea* of what he does; getting from the start some intellectual conception that enters into his practice and enriches it; while every idea finds, directly or indirectly, some application in experience, and has some effect upon life. This, I need hardly say, fixes the position of the "book" or reading in education. Harmful as a substitute for experience, it is all-important in interpreting and expanding experience.

The other chart (IV) illustrates precisely the same idea. It gives the symbolic upper story of this ideal school. In the upper corners are the laboratories; in the lower corners are the studios for art work, both the graphic and auditory arts. The questions, the chemical and physical problems, arising in the kitchen and shop, are taken to the laboratories to be worked out. For instance, this past week one of the older groups of children doing practical

* B? *M.S.D.*

Chart IV

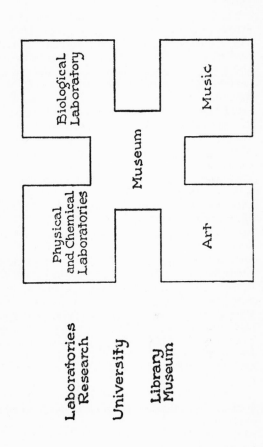

work in weaving which involved the use of the spinning wheel, worked out the diagrams of the direction of forces concerned in treadle and wheel, and the ratio of velocities between wheel and spindle. In the same manner, the plants with which the child has to do in cooking, afford the basis for a concrete interest in botany, and may be taken and studied by themselves. In a certain school in Boston science work for months was centered in the growth of the cotton plant, and yet something new was brought in every day. We hope to do similar work with all the types of plants that furnish materials for sewing and weaving. These examples will suggest, I hope, the relation which the laboratories bear to the rest of the school.

The drawing and music, or the graphic and auditory arts, represent the culmination, the idealization, the highest point of refinement of all the work carried on. I think everybody who has not a purely literary view of the subject recognizes that genuine art grows out of the work of the artisan. The art of the Renaissance was great, because it grew out of the manual arts of life. It did not spring up in a separate atmosphere, however ideal, but carried on to their spiritual meaning processes found in homely and everyday forms of life. The school should observe this relationship. The merely artisan side is narrow, but the mere art, taken by itself, and grafted on from without, tends to become forced, empty, sentimental. I do not mean, of course, that all art work must be correlated in detail to the other work of the school, but simply that a spirit of union gives vitality to the art, and depth and richness to the other work. All art involves physical organs, the eye and hand, the ear and voice; and yet it is something more than the mere technical skill required by the organs of expression. It involves an idea, a thought, a spiritual rendering of things; and yet it is other than any number of ideas by themselves. It is a living union of thought and the instrument of expression. This union is symbolized by saying that in the ideal school the art work might be considered to be that of the shops, passed through the alembic of library and museum into action again.

Take the textile room as an illustration of such a synthesis. I am talking about a future school, the one we hope, some time, to have. The basal fact in that room is that it is a workshop, doing actual things in sewing, spinning, and weaving. The children come into immediate connection with the materials, with various fabrics of silk, cotton, linen and wool. Information at once appears in connection with these materials; their origin, history, their adaptation to particular uses, and the machines of various kinds by which the raw materials are utilized. Discipline arises in dealing with the problems involved, both theoretical and practical. Whence does the culture arise? Partly from seeing all these things reflected through the medium of their scientific and historic conditions and associations, whereby the child learns to appreciate them as technical achievements, as thoughts precipitated in action; and partly because of the introduction of the art idea into the room itself. In the ideal school there would be something of this sort: first, a complete industrial museum, giving samples of materials in various stages of manufacture, and the implements, from the simplest to the most complex, used in dealing with them; then a collection of photographs and pictures illustrating the landscapes and the scenes from which the materials come, their native homes, and their places of manufacture. Such a collection would be a vivid and continual lesson in the synthesis of art, science, and industry. There would be, also, samples of the more perfect forms of textile work, as Italian, French, Japanese, and Oriental. There would be objects illustrating motives of design and decoration which have entered into production. Literature would contribute its part in its idealized representation of the world-industries, as the Penelope in the Odyssey—a classic in literature only because the character is an adequate embodiment of a certain industrial phase of social life. So, from Homer down to the present time, there is a continuous procession of related facts which have been translated into terms of art. Music lends its share, from the Scotch song at the wheel to the spinning song of Marguerite, or of Wagner's Senta. The shop becomes a pictured museum, appealing to the eye. It would have not only materials, beautiful woods and designs, but would give a synopsis of the historical evolution of architecture in its drawings and pictures.

Thus I have attempted to indicate how the school may be connected with life so that the experience gained by the child in a familiar, commonplace way is carried over and made use of there, and what the child learns in the school is carried back and applied in everyday life, making the school an organic whole, instead of a composite of isolated parts. The isolation of studies as well as of parts of the school system disappears. Experience has its geographical aspect, its artistic and its literary, its scientific and its historical sides. All studies arise from aspects of the one earth and the one life lived upon it. We do not have a series of stratified earths, one of which is mathematical, another physical, another historical, and so on. We should not live very long in any one taken by itself. We live in a world where all sides are bound together. All studies grow out of relations in the one great common world. When the child lives in varied but concrete and active relationship to this common world, his studies are naturally unified. It will no longer be a problem to correlate studies. The teacher will not have to resort to all sorts of devices to weave a little arithmetic into the history lesson, and the like. Relate the school to life, and all studies are of necessity correlated.

Moreover, if the school is related as a whole to life as a whole, its various aims and ideals—culture, discipline, information, utility—cease to be variants, for one of which we must select one study and for another another. The growth of the child in the direction of social capacity and service, his larger and more vital union with life, becomes the unifying aim; and discipline, culture and information fall into place as phases of this growth.

I wish to say one word more about the relationship of our particular school to the University. The problem is to unify, to organize education, to bring all its various factors together, through putting it as a whole into organic union with everyday life. That which lies back of the pedagogical school of the University is the necessity of working out something to serve as a model for such unification, extending from work beginning with the four-year-old child up through the graduate work of the University. Already we have much help from the University in scientific work planned, sometimes even in detail, by heads of the departments. The graduate student comes to us with his researches and methods, suggesting ideas and problems. The library and museum are at hand. We want to bring all things educational together; to break down the barriers that divide the education of the little child from the instruction of the maturing youth; to identify the lower and the higher education, so that it shall be demonstrated to the eye that there is no lower and higher, but simply education.

Speaking more especially with reference to the pedagogical side of the work: I suppose the oldest university chair of pedagogy in our country is about twenty years old—that of the University of Michigan, founded in the latter seventies. But there are only one or two that have tried to make a connection between theory and practice. They teach for the most part by theory, by lectures, by reference to books, rather than through the actual work of teaching itself. At Columbia, through the Teachers' College, there is an extensive and close connection between the University and the training of teachers. Something has been done in one or two other places along the same line. We want an even more intimate union here, so that the University shall put all its resources at the disposition of the elementary school, contributing to the evolution of valuable subject-matter and right method, while the school in turn will be a laboratory in which the student of education sees theories and ideas demonstrated, tested, criticised, enforced, and the evolution of new truths. We want the school in its relation to the University to be a working model of a unified education.

A word as to the relation of the school to educational

interests generally. I heard once that the adoption of a certain method in use in our school was objected to by a teacher on this ground: "You know that it is an experimental school. They do not work under the same conditions that we are subject to." Now, the purpose of performing an experiment is that other people need not experiment; at least need not experiment so much, may have something definite and positive to go by. An experiment demands particularly favorable conditions in order that results may be reached both freely and securely. It has to work unhampered, with all the needed resources at command. Laboratories lie back of all the great business enterprises of today, back of every great factory, every railway and steamship system. Yet the laboratory is not a business enterprise; it does not aim to secure for itself the conditions of business life, nor does the commercial undertaking repeat the laboratory. There is a difference between working out and testing a new truth, or a new method, and applying it on a wide scale, making it available for the mass of men, making it commercial. But the first thing is to discover the truth, to afford all necessary facilities, for this is the most practical thing in the world in the long run. We do not expect to have other schools literally imitate what we do. A working model is not something to be copied; it is to afford a demonstration of the feasibility of the principle, and of the methods which make it feasible. So (to come back to our own point) we want here to work out the problem of the unity, the organization of the school system in itself, and to do this by relating it so intimately to life as to demonstrate the possibility and necessity of such organization for all education.

The Child and the Curriculum *

---◆---

By 1902, the relations of the Laboratory School with the administration of the University of Chicago had grown strained, and its continuation was in question. There was no doubt, however, about the impact of the ideas developed at the School upon educators in the United States and other countries. For Dewey, the School was but a single experiment pointing the way toward complete educational reform. His pamphlet The Child and the Curriculum *further elucidated the emphasis upon the present experience of the child that was central in the philosophy and practice of the School. Nowhere is Dewey's opposition to the "old" subject-centered curriculum—or to the extremes of the "new" child-centered approach—stated more clearly. One of Dewey's last writings on education while at Chicago, it is also one of the most widely reprinted and translated.*

Profound differences in theory are never gratuitous or invented. They grow out of conflicting elements in a genuine problem—a problem which is genuine just because the elements, taken as they stand, are conflicting. Any significant problem involves conditions that for the moment contradict each other. Solution comes only by getting away from the meaning of terms that is already fixed upon and coming to see the conditions from another point of view, and hence in a fresh light. But this

* Chicago: The University of Chicago Press, 1902, copyright 1902 by the University of Chicago.

reconstruction means travail of thought. Easier than thinking with surrender of already formed ideas and detachment from facts already learned, is just to stick by what is already said, looking about for something with which to buttress it against attack.

Thus sects arise; schools of opinion. Each selects that set of conditions that appeal to it; and then erects them into a complete and independent truth, instead of treating them as a factor in a problem, needing adjustment.

The fundamental factors in the educative process are an immature, undeveloped being; and certain social aims, meanings, values incarnate in the matured experience of the adult. The educative process is the due interaction of these forces. Such a conception of each in relation to the other as facilitates completest and freest interaction is the essence of educational theory.

But here comes the effort of thought. It is easier to see the conditions in their separateness, to insist upon one at the expense of the other, to make antagonists of them, than to discover a reality to which each belongs. The easy thing is to seize upon something in the nature of the child, or upon something in the developed consciousness of the adult, and insist upon *that* as the key to the whole problem. When this happens a really serious practical problem—that of interaction—is transformed into an unreal, and hence insoluble, theoretic problem. Instead of seeing the educative steadily and as a whole, we see conflicting terms. We get the case of the child *vs.* the curriculum; of the individual nature *vs.* social culture. Below all other divisions in pedagogic opinion lies this opposition.

The child lives in a somewhat narrow world of personal contacts. Things hardly come within his experience unless they touch, intimately and obviously, his own well-being, or that of his family and friends. His world is a world of persons with their personal interests, rather than a realm of facts and laws. Not truth, in the sense of conformity to external fact, but affection and sympathy, is its keynote. As against this, the course of study met in the school presents material stretching back indefinitely in time, and extending outward indefinitely into space. The child is taken out of his familiar physical environment, hardly more than a square mile or so in area, into the wide world—yes, and even to the bounds of the solar system. His little span of personal memory and tradition is overlaid with the long centuries of the history of all peoples.

Again, the child's life is an integral, a total one. He passes quickly and readily from one topic to another, as from one spot to another, but is not conscious of transition or break. There is no conscious isolation, hardly conscious distinction. The things that occupy him are held together by the unity of the personal and social interests which his life carries along. Whatever is uppermost in his mind constitutes to him, for the time being, the whole universe. That universe is fluid and fluent; its contents dissolve and re-form with amazing rapidity. But, after all, it is the child's own world. It has the unity and completeness of his own life. He goes to school, and various studies divide and fractionize the world for him. Geography selects, it abstracts and analyzes one set of facts, and from one particular point of view. Arithmetic is another division, grammar another department, and so on indefinitely.

Again, in school each of these subjects is classified. Facts are torn away from their original place in experience and rearranged with reference to some general principle. Classification is not a matter of child experience; things do not come to the individual pigeonholed. The vital ties of affection, the connecting bonds of activity, hold together the variety of his personal experiences. The adult mind is so familiar with the notion of logically ordered facts that it does not recognize—it cannot realize—the amount of separating and reformulating which the facts of direct experience have to undergo before they can appear as a "study," or branch of learning. A principle, for the intellect, has had to be distinguished and defined; facts have had to be interpreted in relation to this principle, not as they are in themselves. They have had to be regathered about a new center which is wholly abstract and ideal. All this means a development of a special intellectual interest. It means ability to view facts impartially and objectively; that is, without reference to their place and meaning in one's own experience. It means capacity to analyze and to synthesize. It means highly matured intellectual habits and the command of a definite technique and apparatus of scientific inquiry. The studies as classified are the product, in a word, of the science of the ages, not of the experience of the child.

These apparent deviations and differences between child and curriculum might be almost indefinitely widened. But we have here sufficiently fundamental divergences: first, the narrow but personal world of the child against the impersonal but infinitely extended world of space and time; second, the unity, the single whole-heartedness of the child's life, and the specializations and divisions of the curriculum; third, an abstract principle of logical classification and arrangement, and the practical and emotional bonds of child life.

From these elements of conflict grow up different educational sects. One school fixes its attention upon the importance of the subject-matter of the curriculum as compared with the contents of the child's own experience. It is as if they said: Is life petty, narrow, and crude? Then studies reveal the great, wide universe with all its fulness and complexity of meaning. Is the life of the child egoistic, self-centered, impulsive? Then in these studies is found an objective universe of truth, law, and order. Is his experience confused, vague, uncertain, at the mercy of the moment's caprice and circumstance? Then studies introduce a world arranged on the basis of eternal and general truth; a world where all is measured and defined. Hence the moral: ignore and minimize the child's individual peculiarities, whims, and experiences. They are what we need to get away from. They are to be obscured or eliminated. As educators our work is precisely to substitute for these superficial and casual affairs stable and well-ordered realities; and these are found in studies and lessons.

Subdivide each topic into studies; each study into lessons; each lesson into specific facts and formulae. Let the child proceed step by step to master each one of these separate parts, and at last he will have covered the entire ground. The road which looks so long when viewed in its entirety, is easily traveled, considered as a series of particular steps. Thus emphasis is put upon the logical subdivisions and consecutions of the subject-matter. Problems of instruction are problems of procuring texts giving logical parts and sequences, and of presenting these portions in class in a similar definite and graded way. Subject-matter furnishes the end, and it determines method. The child is simply the immature being who is to be matured; he is the superficial being who is to be deepened; his is narrow experience which is to be widened. It is his to receive, to accept. His part is fulfilled when he is ductile and docile.

Not so, says the other sect. The child is the starting-point, the center, and the end. His development, his growth, is the ideal. It alone furnishes the standard. To the growth of the child all studies are subservient; they are instruments valued as they serve the needs of growth. Personality, character, is more than subject-matter. Not knowledge or information, but self-realization, is the goal. To possess all the world of knowledge and lose one's own self is as awful a fate in education as in religion. Moreover, subject-matter never can be got into the child from without. Learning is active. It involves reaching out of the mind. It involves organic assimilation starting from within. Literally, we must take our stand with the child and our departure from him. It is he and not the subject-matter which determines both quality and quantity of learning.

The only significant method is the method of the mind as it reaches out and assimilates. Subject-matter is but spiritual food, possible nutritive material. It cannot digest itself; it cannot of its own accord turn into bone and muscle and blood. The source of whatever is dead, mechanical, and formal in schools is found precisely in the subordination of the life and experience of the child to the curriculum. It is because of this that "study" has become a synonym for what is irksome, and a lesson identical with a task.

This fundamental opposition of child and curriculum set up by these two modes of doctrine can be duplicated in a series of other terms. "Discipline" is the watchword of those who magnify the course of study; "interest" that of those who blazon "The Child" upon their banner. The standpoint of the former is logical; that of the latter psychological. The first emphasizes the necessity of adequate training and scholarship on the part of the teacher; the latter that of need of sympathy with the child, and knowledge of his natural instincts. "Guidance and control" are the catchwords of one school; "freedom and initiative" of the other. Law is asserted here; spontaneity proclaimed there. The old, the conservation of what has been achieved in the pain and toil of the ages, is dear to the one; the new, change, progress, wins the affection of the other. Inertness and routine, chaos and anarchism, are accusations bandied back and forth. Neglect of the sacred authority of duty is charged by one side, only to be met by counter-charges of suppression of individuality through tyrannical despotism.

Such oppositions are rarely carried to their logical conclusion. Common-sense recoils at the extreme character of these results. They are left to theorists, while common-sense vibrates back and forward in a maze of inconsistent compromise. The need of getting theory and practical common-sense into closer connection suggests a return to our original thesis: that we have here conditions which are necessarily related to each other in the educative process, since this is precisely one of interaction and adjustment.

What, then, is the problem? It is just to get rid of the prejudicial notion that there is some gap in kind (as distinct from degree) between the child's experience and the various forms of subject-matter that make up the course of study. From the side of the child, it is a question of seeing how his experience already contains within itself elements—facts and truths—of just the same sort as those entering into the formulated study; and, what is of more importance, of how it contains within itself the attitudes, the motives, and the interests which have operated in developing and organizing the subject-matter to the plane which it now occupies. From the side of the studies, it is a question of interpreting them as outgrowths of forces operating in the child's life, and of discovering the steps that intervene between the child's present experience and their richer maturity.

Abandon the notion of subject-matter as something fixed and ready-made in itself, outside the child's experience; cease thinking of the child's experience as also something hard and fast; see it as something fluent, embryonic, vital; and we realize that the child and the curriculum are simply two limits which define a single process. Just as two points define a straight line, so the present standpoint of the child and the facts and truths of studies define instruction. It is continuous reconstruction, moving from the child's present experience out into that represented by the organized bodies of truth that we call studies.

On the face of it, the various studies, arithmetic, geography, language, botany, etc., are themselves experience —they are that of the race. They embody the cumulative outcome of the efforts, the strivings, and successes of the human race generation after generation. They present this, not as a mere accumulation, not as a miscellaneous heap of separate bits of experience, but in some organized and systematized way—that is, as reflectively formulated.

Hence, the facts and truths that enter into the child's present experience, and those contained in the subject-matter of studies, are the initial and final terms of one reality. To oppose one to the other is to oppose the infancy and maturity of the same growing life; it is to set the moving tendency and the final result of the same process over against each other; it is to hold that the nature and the destiny of the child war with each other.

If such be the case, the problem of the relation of the child and the curriculum presents itself in this guise:

Of what use, educationally speaking, is it to be able to see the end in the beginning? How does it assist us in dealing with the early stages of growth to be able to anticipate its later phases? The studies, as we have agreed, represent the possibilities of development inherent in the child's immediate crude experience. But, after all, they are not parts of that present and immediate life. Why, then, or how, make account of them?

Asking such a question suggests its own answer. To see the outcome is to know in what direction the present experience is moving, provided it move normally and soundly. The far-away point, which is of no significance to us simply as far away, becomes of huge importance the moment we take it as defining a present direction of movement. Taken in this way it is no remote and distant result to be achieved, but a guiding method in dealing with the present. The systematized and defined experience of the adult mind, in other words, is of value to us in interpreting the child's life as it immediately shows itself, and in passing on to guidance or direction.

Let us look for a moment at these two ideas: interpretation and guidance. The child's present experience is in no way self-explanatory. It is not final, but transitional. It is nothing complete in itself, but just a sign or index of certain growth-tendencies. As long as we confine our gaze to what the child here and now puts forth, we are confused and misled. We cannot read its meaning. Extreme depreciations of the child morally and intellectually, and sentimental idealizations of him, have their root in a common fallacy. Both spring from taking stages of a growth or movement as something cut off and fixed. The first fails to see the promise contained in feelings and deeds which, taken by themselves, are unpromising and repellant; the second fails to see that even the most pleasing and beautiful exhibitions are but signs, and that they begin to spoil and rot the moment they are treated as achievements.

What we need is something which will enable us to interpret, to appraise, the elements in the child's present puttings forth and fallings away, his exhibitions of power and weakness, in the light of some larger growth-process in which they have their place. Only in this way can we discriminate. If we isolate the child's present inclinations, purposes, and experiences from the place they occupy and the part they have to perform in a developing experience, all stand upon the same level; all alike are equally good and equally bad. But in the movement of life different elements stand upon different planes of value. Some of the child's deeds are symptoms of a waning tendency; they are survivals in functioning of an organ which has done its part and is passing out of vital use. To give positive attention to such qualities is to arrest development upon a lower level. It is systematically to maintain a rudimentary phase of growth. Other activities are signs of a culminating power and interest; to them applies the maxim of striking while the iron is hot. As regards them, it is perhaps a matter of now or never. Selected, utilized, emphasized, they may mark a turning-point for good in the child's whole career; neglected, an opportunity goes, never to be recalled. Other acts and feelings are prophetic; they represent the dawning of flickering light that will shine steadily only in the far future. As regards them there is little at present to do but give them fair and full chance, waiting for the future for definite direction.

Just as, upon the whole, it was the weakness of the "old education" that it made invidious comparisons between the immaturity of the child and the maturity of the adult, regarding the former as something to be got away from as soon as possible and as much as possible; so it is the danger of the "new education" that it regard the child's present powers and interests as something finally significant in themselves. In truth, his learnings and achievements are fluid and moving. They change from day to day and from hour to hour.

It will do harm if child-study leave in the popular mind the impression that a child of a given age has a positive equipment of purposes and interests to be cultivated just as they stand. Interests in reality are but attitudes toward possible experiences; they are not achievements; their worth is in the leverage they afford, not in the accomplishment they represent. To take the phenomena presented at a given age as in any way self-explanatory or self-contained is inevitably to result in indulgence and spoiling. Any power, whether of child or adult, is indulged when it is taken on its given and present level in consciousness. Its genuine meaning is in the propulsion it affords toward a higher level. It is just something to do with. Appealing to the interest upon the present plane means excitation; it means playing with a power so as continually to stir it up without directing it toward definite achievement. Continuous initiation, continuous starting of activities that do not arrive, is, for all practical purposes, as bad as the continual repression of initiative in conformity with supposed interests of some more perfect thought or will. It is as if the child were forever tasting and never eating; always having his palate tickled upon the emotional side, but never getting the organic satisfaction that comes only with the digestion of food and transformation of it into working power.

As against such a view, the subject-matter of science and history and art serves to reveal the real child to us. We do not know the meaning either of his tendencies or of his performances excepting as we take them as germinating seed, or opening bud, of some fruit to be borne. The whole world of visual nature is all too small an answer to the problem of the meaning of the child's instinct for light and form. The entire science of physics is none too much to interpret adequately to us what is involved in some simple demand of the child for explanation of some casual change that has attracted his attention. The art of Rafael or of Corot is none too much to enable us to value the impulses stirring in the child when he draws and daubs.

So much for the use of the subject-matter in interpretation. Its further employment in direction or guidance is but an expansion of the same thought. To interpret the fact is to see it in its vital movement, to see it in its relation to growth. But to view it as a part of a normal growth is to secure the basis for guiding it. Guidance is not external imposition. *It is freeing the life-process for its own most adequate fulfilment.* What was said about disregard of the child's present experience because of its remoteness from mature experience; and of the sentimental idealization of the child's naïve caprices and performances, may be repeated here with slightly altered phrase. There are those who see no alternative between forcing the child from without, or leaving him entirely alone. Seeing no alternative, some choose one mode, some another. Both fall into the same fundamental error. Both fail to see that development is a definite process, having its own law which can be fulfilled only when adequate and normal conditions are provided. Really to interpret the child's present crude impulses in counting, measuring, and arranging things in rhythmic series, involves mathematical scholarship—a knowledge of the mathematical formulae and relations which have, in the history of the race, grown out of just such crude beginnings. To see the whole history of development which intervenes between these two terms is simply to see what step the child needs to take just here and now; to what use he needs to put his blind impulse in order that it may get clarity and gain force.

If, once more, the "old education" tended to ignore the dynamic quality, the developing force inherent in the child's present experience, and therefore to assume that direction and control were just matters of arbitrarily putting the child in a given path and compelling him to walk there, the "new education" is in danger of taking the idea of development in altogether too formal and empty a way. The child is expected to "develop" this or that fact or truth out of his own mind. He is told to think things out, or work things out for himself, without being supplied any of the environing conditions which are requisite to start and guide thought. Nothing can be developed from nothing; nothing but the crude can be developed out of the crude—and this is what surely happens when we throw the child back upon his achieved self as a finality, and invite him to spin new truths of nature or of conduct out of that. It is certainly as futile to expect a child to evolve a universe out of his own mere mind as it is for a philosopher to attempt that task. Development does not mean just getting something out of the mind. It is a development of experience and into experience that is really wanted. And this is impossible save as just that educative medium is provided which will enable the powers and interests that have been selected as valuable to function. They must operate, and how they operate will depend almost entirely upon the stimuli which surround them, and the material upon which they exercise themselves. The problem of direction is thus the problem of selecting appropriate stimuli for instincts and impulses which it is desired to employ in the gaining of new experience. What new experiences are desirable, and thus what stimuli are needed, it is impossible to tell except as there is some comprehension of the development which is aimed at; except, in a word, as the adult knowledge is drawn upon as revealing the possible career open to the child.

It may be of use to distinguish and to relate to each other the logical and the psychological aspects of experience—the former standing for subject-matter in itself, the latter for it in relation to the child. A psychological statement of experience follows its actual growth; it is historic; it notes steps actually taken, the uncertain and tortuous, as well as the efficient and successful. The logical point of view, on the other hand, assumes that the development has reached a certain positive stage of fulfilment. It neglects the process and considers the outcome. It summarizes and arranges, and thus separates the achieved results from the actual steps by which they were forthcoming in the first instance. We may compare the difference between the logical and the psychological to the difference between the notes which an explorer makes in a new country, blazing a trail and finding his way along as best he may, and the finished map that is constructed after the country has been thoroughly explored. The two are mutually dependent. Without the more or less accidental and devious paths traced by the explorer there would be no facts which could be utilized in the making of the complete and related chart. But no one would get the benefit of the explorer's trip if it was not compared and checked up with similar wanderings undertaken by others; unless the new geographical facts learned, the streams crossed, the mountains climbed, etc., were viewed, not as mere incidents in the journey of the particular traveler, but (quite apart from the individual explorer's life) in relation to other similar facts already known. The map orders individual experiences, connecting them with one another irrespective of the local and temporal circumstances and accidents of their original discovery.

Of what use is this formulated statement of experience? Of what use is the map?

Well, we may first tell what the map is not. The map is not a substitute for a personal experience. The map does not take the place of an actual journey. The logically formulated material of a science or branch of learning, of a study, is no substitute for the having of individual experiences. The mathematical formula for a falling body does not take the place of personal contact and immediate individual experience with the falling thing. But the map, a summary, an arranged and orderly view of previous experiences, serves as a guide to future experience; it gives direction; it facilitates control; it economizes effort, preventing useless wandering, and pointing out the paths which lead most quickly and most certainly to a desired result. Through the map every new traveler may get for his own journey the benefits of the results of others' explorations without the waste of energy and loss of time involved in their wanderings—wanderings which he himself would be obliged to repeat were it not for just the assistance of the objective and generalized record of their performances. That which we call a science or study puts the net product of past experience in the form which makes it most available for the future. It represents a capitalization which may at once be turned to interest. It economizes the workings of the mind in every way. Memory is less taxed because the facts are grouped together about some common principle, instead of being connected solely with the varying incidents of their original discovery. Observation is assisted; we know what to look for and where to look. It is the difference between looking for a needle in a haystack, and searching for a given paper in a well-arranged cabinet. Reasoning is directed, because there is a certain general path or line laid out along which ideas naturally march, instead of moving from one chance association to another.

There is, then, nothing final about a logical rendering of experience. Its value is not contained in itself; its significance is that of standpoint, outlook, method. It intervenes between the more casual, tentative, and roundabout experiences of the past, and more controlled and orderly experiences of the future. It gives past experience in that net form which renders it most available and most significant, most fecund for future experience. The abstractions, generalizations, and classifications which it introduces all have prospective meaning.

The formulated result is then not to be opposed to the process of growth. The logical is not set over against the psychological. The surveyed and arranged result occupies a critical position in the process of growth. It marks a turning-point. It shows how we may get the benefit of past effort in controlling future endeavor. In the largest sense the logical standpoint is itself psychological; it has its meaning as a point in the development of experience, and its justification is in its functioning in the future growth which it insures.

Hence the need of reinstating into experience the subject-matter of the studies, or branches of learning. It must be restored to the experience from which it has been abstracted. It needs to be *psychologized;* turned over, translated into the immediate and individual experiencing within which it has its origin and significance.

Every study or subject thus has two aspects: one for the scientist as a scientist; the other for the teacher as a teacher. These two aspects are in no sense opposed or conflicting. But neither are they immediately identical.

For the scientist, the subject-matter represents simply a given body of truth to be employed in locating new problems, instituting new researches, and carrying them through to a verified outcome. To him the subject-matter of the science is self-contained. He refers various portions of it to each other; he connects new facts with it. He is not, as a scientist, called upon to travel outside its particular bounds; if he does, it is only to get more facts of the same general sort. The problem of the teacher is a different one. As a teacher he is not concerned with adding new facts to the science he teaches; in propounding new hypotheses or in verifying them. He is concerned with the subject-matter of the science as *representing a given stage and phase of the development of experience.* His problem is that of inducing a vital and personal experiencing. Hence, what concerns him, as teacher, is the ways in which that subject may become a part of experience; what there is in the child's present that is usable with reference to it; how such elements are to be used; how his own knowledge of the subject-matter may assist in interpreting the child's needs and doings, and determine the medium in which the child should be placed in order that his growth may be properly directed. He is concerned, not with the subject-matter as such, but with the subject-matter as a related factor in a total and growing experience. Thus to see it is to psychologize it.

It is the failure to keep in mind the double aspect of subject-matter which causes the curriculum and child to be set over against each other as described in our early pages. The subject-matter, just as it is for the scientist, has no direct relationship to the child's present experience. It stands outside of it. The danger here is not a merely theoretical one. We are practically threatened on all sides. Text-book and teacher vie with each other in presenting to the child the subject-matter as it stands to the specialist. Such modification and revision as it undergoes are a mere elimination of certain scientific difficulties, and the general reduction to a lower intellectual level. The material is not translated into life-terms, but is directely offered as a substitute for, or an external annex to, the child's present life.

Three typical evils result: In the first place, the lack of any organic connection with what the child has already seen and felt and loved makes the material purely formal and symbolic. There is a sense in which it is impossible to value too highly the formal and the symbolic. The genuine form, the real symbol, serve as methods in the holding and discovery of truth. They are tools by which the individual pushes out most surely and widely into unexplored areas. They are means by which he brings to bear whatever of reality he has succeeded in gaining in past searchings. But this happens only when the symbol really symbolizes—when it stands for and sums up in shorthand actual experiences which the individual has already gone through. A symbol which is induced from without, which has not been led up to in preliminary activities, is, as we say, a *bare* or *mere* symbol; it is dead and barren. Now, any fact, whether of arithmetic, or geography, or grammar, which is not led up to and into out of something which has previously occupied a significant position in the child's life for its own sake, is forced into this position. It is not a reality, but just the sign of a reality which *might* be experienced if certain conditions were fulfilled. But the abrupt presentation of the fact as something known by others, and requiring only to be studied and learned by the child, rules out such conditions of fulfilment. It condemns the fact to be hieroglyph: it would mean something if one only had the key. The clue being lacking, it remains an idle curiosity, to fret and obstruct the mind, a dead weight to burden it.

The second evil in this external presentation is lack of motivation. There are not only no facts or truths which have been previously felt as such with which to appropriate and assimilate the new, but there is no craving, no need, no demand. When the subject-matter has been psychologized, that is, viewed as an outgrowth of present tendencies and activities, it is easy to locate in the present some obstacle, intellectual, practical, or ethical, which can be handled more adequately if the truth in question be mastered. This need supplies motive for the learning. An end which is the child's own carries him on to possess the means of its accomplishment. But when material is directly supplied in the form of a lesson to be learned as a lesson, the connecting links of need and aim are conspicuous for their absence. What we mean by the mechanical and dead in instruction is a result of this lack of motivation. The organic and vital mean interaction—they mean play of mental demand and material supply.

The third evil is that even the most scientific matter, arranged in most logical fashion, loses this quality, when presented in external, ready-made fashion, by the time it gets to the child. It has to undergo some modification in order to shut out some phases too hard to grasp, and to reduce some of the attendant difficulties. What happens? Those things which are most significant to the scientific man, and most valuable in the logic of actual inquiry and classification, drop out. The really thought-provoking character is obscured, and the organizing function disappears. Or, as we commonly say, the child's reasoning powers, the faculty of abstraction and generalization, are not adequately developed. So the subject-matter is evacuated of its logical value, and, though it is what it is only from the logical standpoint, is presented as stuff only for "memory." This is the contradiction: the child gets the advantage neither of the adult logical formulation, nor of his own native competencies of apprehension and response. Hence the logic of the child is hampered and mortified, and we are almost fortunate if he does not get actual non-science, flat and commonplace residua of what was gaining scientific vitality a generation or two ago—degenerate reminiscence of what someone else once formulated on the basis of the experience that some further person had, once upon a time, experienced.

The train of evils does not cease. It is all too common for opposed erroneous theories to play straight into each other's hands. Psychological considerations may be slurred or shoved one side; they cannot be crowded out. Put out of the door, they come back through the window. Somehow and somewhere motive must be appealed to, connection must be established between the mind and its material. There is no question of getting along without this bond of connection; the only question is whether it be such as grows out of the material itself in relation to the mind, or be imported and hitched on from some outside source. If the subject-matter of the lessons be such as to have an appropriate place within the expanding consciousness of the child, if it grows out of his own past doings, thinkings, and sufferings, and grows into application in further achievements and receptivities, then no device or trick of method has to be resorted to in order to enlist "interest." The psychologized *is* of interest—that is, it is placed in the whole of conscious life so that it shares the worth of that life. But the externally presented material, that, conceived and generated in standpoints and attitudes remote from the child, and developed in motives alien to him, has no such place of its own. Hence the recourse to adventitious leverage to push it in, to factitious drill to drive it in, to artificial bribe to lure it in.

Three aspects of this recourse to outside ways for giving the subject-matter some psychological meaning may be worth mentioning. Familiarity breeds contempt, but it also breeds something like affection. We get used to the chains we wear, and we miss them when removed. 'Tis an old story that through custom we finally embrace what at first wore a hideous mien. Unpleasant, because meaningless, activities may get agreeable if long enough persisted in. *It is possible for the mind to develop interest in a routine or mechanical procedure, if conditions are continually supplied which demand that mode of operation and preclude any other sort.* I frequently hear dulling devices and empty exercises defended and extolled because "the children take such an 'interest' in them." Yes, that is the worst of it; the mind, shut out from worthy employ and missing the taste of adequate performance, comes down to the level of that which is left to it to know and do, and perforce takes an interest in a cabined and cramped experience. To find satisfaction in its own exercise is the normal law of mind, and if large and meaningful business for the mind be denied, it tries to content itself with the formal movements that remain to it—and too often succeeds, save in those cases of more intense activity which cannot accommodate themselves, and that make up the unruly and *declassé* of our school product. An interest in the formal apprehension of symbols and in their memorized reproduction becomes in many pupils a substitute for the original and vital interest in reality; and all because, the subject-matter of the course of study being out of relation to the concrete mind of the individual, some substitute bond to hold it in some kind of working relation to the mind must be discovered and elaborated.

The second substitute for living motivation in the subject-matter is that of contrast-effects; the material of the lesson is rendered interesting, if not in itself, at least in contrast with some alternative experience. To learn the lesson is more interesting than to take a scolding, be held up to general ridicule, stay after school, receive degradingly low marks, or fail to be promoted. And very much of what goes by the name of "discipline," and prides itself upon opposing the doctrines of a soft pedagogy and upon upholding the banner of effort and duty, is nothing more or less than just this appeal to "interest" in its obverse aspect—to fear, to dislike of various kinds of physical, social, and personal pain. The subject-matter does not appeal; it cannot appeal; it lacks origin and bearing in a growing experience. So the appeal is to the thousand and one outside and irrelevant agencies which may serve to throw, by sheer rebuff and rebound, the mind back upon the material from which it is constantly wandering.

Human nature being what it is, however, it tends to seek its motivation in the agreeable rather than in the disagreeable, in direct pleasure rather than in alternative pain. And so has come up the modern theory and practice of the "interesting," in the false sense of that term.

The material is still left; so far as its own characteristics are concerned, just material externally selected and formulated. It is still just so much geography and arithmetic and grammar study; not so much potentiality of child-experience with regard to language, earth, and numbered and measured reality. Hence the difficulty of bringing the mind to bear upon it; hence its repulsiveness; the tendency for attention to wander; for other acts and images to crowd in and expel the lesson. The legitimate way out is to transform the material; to psychologize it—that is, once more, to take it and to develop it within the range and scope of the child's life. But it is easier and simpler to leave it as it is, and then by trick of method to *arouse* interest, to *make* it *interesting;* to cover it with sugar-coating; to conceal its barrenness by intermediate and unrelated material; and finally, as it were, to get the child to swallow and digest the unpalatable morsel while he is enjoying tasting something quite different. But alas for the analogy! Mental assimilation is a matter of consciousness; and if the attention has not been playing upon the actual material, that has not been apprehended, nor worked into faculty.

How, then, stands the case of Child *vs.* Curriculum? What shall the verdict be? The radical fallacy in the original pleadings with which we set out is the supposition that we have no choice save either to leave the child to his own unguided spontaneity or to inspire direction upon him from without. Action is response; it is adaptation, adjustment. There is no such thing as sheer self-activity possible—because all activity takes place in a medium, in a situation, and with reference to its conditions. But, again, no such thing as imposition of truth from without, as insertion of truth from without, is possible. All depends upon the activity which the mind itself undergoes in responding to what is presented from without. Now, the value of the formulated wealth of knowledge that makes up the course of study is that it may enable the educator *to determine the environment of the child,* and thus by indirection to direct. Its primary value, its primary indication, is for the teacher, not for the child. It says to the teacher: Such and such are the capacities, the fulfilments, in truth and beauty and behavior, open to these children. Now see to it that day by day the conditions are such that *their own activities* move inevitably in this direction, toward such culmination of themselves. Let the child's nature fulfil its own destiny, revealed to you in whatever of science and art and industry the world now holds as its own.

The case is of Child. It is his present powers which are to assert themselves; his present capacities which are to be exercised; his present attitudes which are to be realized. But save as the teacher knows, knows wisely and thoroughly, the race-experience which is embodied in that thing we call the Curriculum, the teacher knows neither what the present power, capacity, or attitude is, nor yet how it is to be asserted, exercised, and realized.

Progressive Education and the Science of Education*

Dewey became deeply disturbed over some of the ideas and programs that were called "progressive" in education—especially in the decade following the First World War, when notions of educational reform were increasingly affected by the alternating extravagances of hope and sentimental disillusionment that characterized the era. After refusing to involve himself with the Progressive Education Association, which had been founded in 1919, Dewey accepted an honorary presidency in 1928—and used the occasion to speak out for intellectual rigor necessary if the progressive movement was to make a contribution to a science of education. Dewey's doubts and warnings had little effect upon those who called themselves his followers. As this address may illustrate, he may have been reluctant to appear too stringently critical of what he regarded as part of a necessary movement toward reform. More fundamental, however, is the question whether it was the ambiguities of his own philosophy that had encouraged the oversimplifications and exaggerations which he condemned.

What is Progressive Education? What is the meaning of experiment in education, of an experimental school? What can such schools as are represented here do for other schools, in which the great, indefinitely the greater, number of children receive their instruction and disci-

* *Progressive Education*, Vol. V (1928), pp. 197-204. Reprinted by permission of the Committee on Publications of the John Dewey Society.

pline? What can be rightfully expected from the work of these progressive schools in the way of a contribution to intelligent and stable educational practice; especially what can be expected in the way of a contribution to educational theory? Are there common elements, intellectual and moral, in the various undertakings here represented? Or is each school going its own way, having for its foundation the desires and preferences of the particular person who happens to be in charge? Is experimentation a process of trying anything at least once, of putting into immediate effect any "happy thought" that comes to mind, or does it rest upon principles which are adopted at least as a working hypothesis? Are actual results consistently observed and used to check an underlying hypothesis so that the latter develops intellectually? Can we be content if from the various progressive schools there emanate suggestions which radiate to other schools to enliven and vitalize their work; or should we demand that out of the cooperative undertakings of the various schools a coherent body of educational principles shall gradually emerge as a distinctive contribution to the theory of education?

Such questions as these come to mind on the occasion of such a gathering as this. The interrogations expressed are far from all inclusive. They are one-sided, and intentionally so. They glide over the important questions that may be asked about what these schools are actually doing for the children who attend them; how they are meeting their primary responsibility that to the children themselves and their families and friends. The one-sided emphasis is, as was said, intentional. The questions are shaped to take another slant; to direct attention to the intellectual contribution to be expected of progressive schools. The reasons for this one-sidedness are close at hand. It is natural that in your own exchange of experiences and ideas the question slurred over should be prominent. And that pupils in progressive schools are themselves progressing, and that the movement to establish more progressive schools is progressing, I have no doubt. Nor do I think that the old question, once a bugaboo, as to what will happen when the pupils go to college or out into life, is any longer an open one. Experience has proved that they give a good account of themselves; so it has seemed to me that the present is a fitting time to raise the intellectual, the theoretical problem of the relation of the progressive movement to the art and philosophy of education.

The query as to common elements in the various schools receives an easy answer up to a certain point. All of the schools, I take it for granted, exhibit as compared with traditional schools, a common emphasis upon respect for individuality and for increased freedom; a common disposition to build upon the nature and experience of the boys and girls that come to them, instead of imposing from without external subject-matter and standards. They all display a certain atmosphere of informality, because experience has proved that formalization is hostile to genuine mental activity and to sincere emotional expression and growth. Emphasis upon activity as distinct from passivity is one of the common factors. And again I assume that there is in all of these schools a common unusual attention to the human factors, to normal social relations, to communication and intercourse which is like in kind to that which is found in the great world beyond the school doors; that all alike believe that these normal human contacts of child with child and of child with teacher are of supreme educational importance, and that all alike disbelieve in those artificial personal relations which have been the chief factor in isolation of schools from life. So much at least of common spirit and purpose we may assume to exist. And in so far we already have the elements of a distinctive contribution to the body of educational theory: respect for individual capacities, interests and experience; enough external freedom and informality at least to enable teachers to become acquainted with children as they really are; respect for self-initiated and self-conducted learning; respect for activity as the stimulus and centre of learning; and perhaps above all belief in social contact, communication, and coöperation upon a normal human plane as all-enveloping medium.

These ideas constitute no mean contribution: It is a contribution to educational theory as well as to the happiness and integrity of those who come under the influence of progressive schools. But the elements of the contribution are general, and like all generalities subject to varied and ambiguous interpretations. They indicate the starting point of the contribution that progressive schools may make to the theory or science of education, but only the starting point. Let us then reduce our questions to a single one and ask, What is the distinctive relation of progressive education to the science of education, understanding by science a body of verified facts and tested principles which may give intellectual guidance to the practical operating of schools?

Unless we beg the question at the outset assuming that it is already known just what education is, just what are its aims and what are its methods, there is nothing false nor extravagant in declaring that at the present time different sciences of education are not only possible but also much needed. Of course such a statement goes contrary to the idea that science by its very nature is a single and universal system of truths. But this idea need not frighten us. Even in the advanced sciences, like those of mathematics and physics, advance is made by entertaining different points of view and hypotheses, and working upon different theories. The sciences present no fixed and closed orthodoxy.

And certainly in such an undertaking as education, we must employ the word "science" modestly and humbly; there is no subject in which the claim to be strictly scientific is more likely to suffer from pretense, and none in which it is more dangerous to set up a rigid orthodoxy, a standardized set of beliefs to be accepted by all. Since there is no one *thing* which is beyond question, education, and since there is no likelihood that there will be until society and hence schools have reached a dead monotonous uniformity of practice and aim, there cannot be one single science. As the working operations of schools differ, so must the intellectual theories devised from those operations. Since the practice of progressive education differs from that of the traditional schools, it would be absurd to suppose that the intellectual formulation and organization which fits one type will hold for the other. To be genuine, the science which springs from schools of the older and traditional type, must work upon that foundation, and endeavor to reduce its subject-matter and methods to principles such that their adoption will eliminate waste, conserve resources, and render the existing type of practice more effective. In the degree in which progressive schools mark a departure in their emphasis from old standards, as they do in freedom, individuality, activity, and a coöperative social medium the intellectual organization, the body of facts and principles which they may contribute must of necessity be different. At most they can only occasionally borrow from the "science" that is evolved on the basis of a different type of practice, and they can even then borrow only what is appropriate to their own special aims and processes. To discover how much is relevant is of course a real problem. But this is a very different thing from assuming that the methods and results obtained under traditional scholastic conditions form the standard of science to which progressive schools must conform.

For example it is natural and proper that the theory of the practices found in traditional schools should set great store by tests and measurements. This theory reflects modes of school administration in which marks, grading, classes, and promotions are important. Measurement of I.Qs and achievements are ways of making these operations more efficient. It would not be hard to show that need for classification underlies the importance of testing for I.Qs. The aim is to establish a norm. The norm, omitting statistical refinements, is essentially an average found by taking a sufficiently large number of persons. When this average is found, any given child can be rated. He comes up to it, falls below it, or exceeds it, by an assignable quantity. Thus the application of the results make[s] possible a more precise classification than did older methods which were by comparison hit and miss. But what has all this to do with schools where individuality is a primary object of consideration, and wherein the so-called "class" becomes a grouping for social purposes and wherein diversity of ability and experience rather than uniformity is prized?

In the averaging and classificatory scheme some special capacity, say in music, dramatics, drawing, mechanical skill or any other art, appears only one along with a large number of other factors, or perhaps does not appear at all in the list of things tested. In any case, it figures in the final result only as smoothed down, ironed out, against a large number of other factors. In the progressive school, such an ability is a distinctive resource to be utilized in the coöperative experience of a group; to level it down by averaging it with other qualities until it simply counts in assigning to the individual child a determinate point on a curve is simply hostile to the aim and spirit of progressive schools.

Nor need the progressive educator be unduly scared by the idea that science is constituted by quantitative results, and, as it is often said, that whatever exists can be measured, for all subjects pass through a qualitative stage before they arrive at a quantitative one; and if this were the place it could be shown that even in the mathematical sciences quantity occupies a secondary place as compared with ideas of order which verge on the qualitative. At all events, *quality* of activity and of consequence is more important for the teacher than any quantitative element. If this fact prevents the development of a certain kind of science, it may be unfortunate. But the educator cannot sit down and wait till there are methods by which quality may be reduced to quantity; he must operate here and now. If he can organize his qualitative processes and results into some connected intellectual form, he is really advancing scientific method much more than if, ignoring what is actually most important, he devotes his energies to such unimportant by-products as may now be measured.

Moreover, even if it be true that everything which

exists could be measured—if only we knew how—that which does *not* exist cannot be measured. And it is no paradox to say that the teacher is deeply concerned with what does not exist. For a progressive school is primarily concerned with growth, with a moving and changing process, with *transforming* existing capacities and experiences; what already exists by way of native endowment and past achievement is subordinate to what it may become. Possibilities are more important than what already exists, and knowledge of the latter counts only in its bearing upon possibilities. The place of measurement of achievements as a theory of education is very different in a static educational system from what it is in one which is dynamic, or in which the ongoing process of growing is the important thing.

The same principle applies to the attempt to determine objectives and select subject-matter of studies by wide collection and accurate measurement of data. If we are satisfied upon the whole with the aims and processes of existing society, this method is appropriate. If you want schools to perpetuate the present order, with at most an elimination of waste and with such additions as enable it to do better what it is already doing, then one type of intellectual method or "science" is indicated. But if one conceives that a social order different in quality and direction from the present is desirable and that schools should strive to educate with social change in view by producing individuals not complacent about what already exists, and equipped with desires and abilities to assist in transforming it, quite a different method and content is indicated for educational science.

While what has been said may have a tendency to relieve educators in progressive schools from undue anxiety about the criticism that they are unscientific—a criticism levelled from the point of view of theory appropriate to schools of quite a different purpose and procedure—it is not intended to exempt them from responsibility for contributions of an organized, systematic, intellectual quality. The contrary is the case. All new and reforming movements pass through a stage in which what is most evident is a negative phase, one of protest, of deviation, and innovation. It would be surprising indeed if this were not true of the progressive educational movement. For instance, the formality and fixity of traditional schools seemed oppressive, restrictive. Hence in a school which departs from these ideals and methods, freedom is at first most naturally conceived as removal of artificial and benumbing restrictions. Removal, abolition are, however, negative things, so in time it comes to be seen that such freedom is no end in itself, nothing to be satisfied with and to stay by, but marks at most an opportunity to do something of a positive and constructive sort.

Now I wonder whether this earlier and more negative phase of progressive education has not upon the whole run its course, and whether the time has not arrived in which these schools are undertaking a more constructively organized function. One thing is sure: in the degree in which they enter upon organized constructive work, they are bound to make definite contributions to building up the theoretical or intellectual side of education. Whether this be called science or philosophy of education, I for one, care little; but if they do not *intellectually* organize their own work, while they may do much in making the lives of the children committed to them more joyous and more vital, they contribute only incidental scraps to the science of education.

The word organization has been freely used. This word suggests the nature of the problem. Organization and administration are words associated together in the traditional scheme, hence organization conveys the idea of something external and set. But reaction from this sort of organization only creates a demand for another sort. Any genuine intellectual organization is flexible and moving, but it does not lack its own internal principles of order and continuity. An experimental school is under the temptation to improvise its subject-matter. It must take advantage of unexpected events and turn to account unexpected questions and interests. Yet if it permits improvisation to dictate its course, the result is a jerky, discontinuous movement which works against the possibility of making any important contribution to educational subject-matter. Incidents are momentary, but the use made of them should not be momentary or short-lived. They are to be brought within the scope of a developing whole of content and purpose, which is a whole because it has continuity and consecutiveness in its parts. There is no single subject-matter which all schools must adopt, but in every school there should be some significant subject-matters undergoing growth and formulation.

An illustration may help make clearer what is meant. Progressive schools set store by individuality, and sometimes it seems to be thought that orderly organization of subject-matter is hostile to the needs of students in their individual character. But individuality is something developing and to be continuously attained, not something given all at once and ready-made. It is found only in life-history, in its continuing growth; it is, so to say, a career and not just a fact discoverable at a particular cross section of life. It is quite possible for teachers to make such a fuss over individual children, worrying about their peculiarities, their likes and dislikes, their weaknesses and failures, so that they miss perception of real individuality, and indeed tend to adopt methods which show no faith in the power of individuality. A child's individuality cannot be found in what he does or in what he consciously likes at a given moment; it can be found only in the connected course of his actions. Consciousness of desire and purpose can be genuinely attained only toward the close of some fairly prolonged sequence of activities. Consequently some organization of subject-matter reached through a serial or consecutive course of doings, held together within the unity of progressively growing occupation or project, is the only means which corresponds to real individuality. So far is organization from being hostile to the principle of individuality.

Thus much of the energy that sometimes goes to thinking about individual children might better be devoted to discovering some worthwhile activity and to arranging the conditions under which it can be carried forward. As a child engages in this consecutive and cumulative occupation, then in the degree in which it contains valuable subject-matter, the realization or building up of his individuality comes about as a consequence, one might truly say, as a natural by-product. He finds and develops himself in what he does, not in isolation but by interaction with the conditions which contain and carry subject-matter. Moreover a teacher can find out immensely more about the real needs, desires, interests, capacities, and weaknesses of a pupil by observing him throughout the course of such consecutive activity than by any amount of direct prodding or of merely cross-sectional observation. And all observations are of necessity cross-sectional when made of a child engaged in a succession of disconnected activities.

Such a succession of unrelated activities does not provide, of course, the opportunity or content of building up an organized subject-matter. But neither do they provide for the development of a coherent and integrated self. Bare doing, no matter how active, is not enough. An activity or project must, of course, be within the range of the experience of pupils and connected with their needs—which is very far from being identical with any likes or desires which they can consciously express. This negative condition having been met, the test of a good project is whether it is sufficiently full and complex to demand a variety of responses from different children and permit each to go at it and make his contribution in a way which is characteristic of himself. The further test or mark of a good activity, educationally speaking, is that it have a sufficiently long time-span so that a series of endeavors and explorations are involved in it, and included in such a way that each step opens up a new field, raises new questions, arouses a demand for further knowledge, and suggests what to do next on the basis of what has been accomplished and the knowledge thereby gained. Occupational activities which meet these two conditions will of necessity result in not only amassing known subject-matter but in its organization. They simply cannot be carried on without resulting in some orderly collection and systematization of related facts and principles. So far is the principle of working toward organization of knowledge not hostile to the principles of progressive education that the latter cannot perform its functions without reaching out into such organization.

An exaggerated illustration, amounting to a caricature, may perhaps make the point clearer. Suppose there is a school in which pupils are surrounded with a wealth of material objects, apparatus, and tools of all sorts. Suppose they are simply asked what they would like to do and then told in effect to "go to it," the teacher keeping hands—and mind, too—off. *What* are they going to do? What assurance is there that what they do is anything more than the expression, and exhaustion, of a momentary impulse and interest? The supposition does not, you may say, correspond to any fact. But what are the implications of the opposite principle? Where can we stop as we get away from the principle contained in the illustration? Of necessity—and this is as true of the traditional school as of a progressive—the start, the first move, the initial impulse in action, must proceed from the pupil. You can lead a horse to water but you can't make him drink. But whence comes his idea of *what* to do? That must come from what he has already heard or seen; or from what he sees some other child doing. It comes as a suggestion from beyond himself, from the environment, he being not an originator of the idea and purpose but a vehicle through which his surroundings past and present suggest something to him. That such suggestions are likely to be chance ideas, soon exhausted, is highly probable. I think observation will show that when a child enters upon a really fruitful and consecutively developing activity, it is because, and in as far as, he has previously engaged in some complex and gradually unfolding activity which has left him a question he wishes to prove further or with the idea of some piece of work still to be accomplished to bring his occupation to completion. Otherwise he is at the mercy of chance suggestion, and chance suggestions are not likely to lead to anything significant or fruitful.

While in outward form, these remarks are given to show that the teacher, as the member of the group having the riper and fuller experience and the greater insight into the possibilities of continuous development found in any suggested project, has not only the right but the duty to suggest lines of activity, and to show that there need not be any fear of adult imposition provided the teacher knows children as well as subjects, their import is not exhausted in bringing out this fact. Their basic purport is to show that progressive schools by virtue of being progressive, and not in spite of that fact, are under the necessity of finding projects which involve an orderly development and inter-connection of subject-matter, since otherwise there can be no sufficiently complex and long-span undertaking. The opportunity and the need impose a responsibility. Progressive teachers may and can work out and present to other teachers for trial and criticism definite and organized bodies of knowledge, together with a listing of sources from which additional information of the same sort can be secured. If it is asked how the presentation of such bodies of knowledge would differ from the standardized texts of traditional schools, the answer is easy. In the first place, the material would be associated with and derived from occupational activities or prolonged courses of action undertaken by the pupils themselves. In the second place, the material presented would not be something to be literally followed by other teachers and students, but would be indications of the intellectual possibilities of this and that course of activity—statements on the basis of carefully directed and observed experience of the questions that have arisen in connection with them and of the kind of information found useful in answering them, and of where that knowledge can be had. No second experience would exactly duplicate the course of the first; but the presentation of material of this kind would liberate and direct the activities of any teacher in dealing with the distinctive emergencies and needs that would arise in re-undertaking the same general type of project. Further material thus developed would be added, and a large and yet free body of related subject-matter would gradually be built up.

As I have touched in a cursory manner upon the surface of a number of topics, it may be well in closing to summarize. In substance, the previous discussion has tried to elicit at least two contributions which progressive schools may make to that type of a science of education which corresponds to their own type of procedure. One is the development of organized subject-matter just spoken of. The other is a study of the conditions favorable to learning. As I have already said there are certain traits characteristic of progressive schools which are not ends in themselves but which are opportunities to be used. These reduce themselves to opportunities for *learning,* for gaining knowledge, mastering definite modes of skill or techniques, and acquiring socially desirable attitudes and habits—the three chief aspects of learning, I should suppose. Now of necessity the contribution from the side of traditional schools to this general topic is concerned chiefly with methods of teaching, or, if it passes beyond that point, to the methods of study adopted by students. But from the standpoint of progressive education, the question of method takes on a new and still largely untouched form. It is no longer a question of how the teacher is to instruct or how the pupil is to study. The problem is to find what conditions must be fulfilled in order that study and learning will naturally and necessarily take place, what conditions must be present so that pupils will make the responses which cannot help having learning as their consequence. The pupil's mind is no longer to be on study or learning. It is given to doing the things that the situation calls for, while learning is the result. The method of the teacher, on the other hand, becomes a matter of finding the conditions which call out self-educative activity, or learning, and of coöperating with the activities of the pupils so that they have learning as their consequence.

A series of constantly multiplying careful reports on conditions which experience has shown in actual cases to be favorable and unfavorable to learning would revolutionize the whole subject of method. The problem is complex and difficult. Learning involves, as just said, at least three factors: knowledge, skill, and character. Each of these must be studied. It requires judgment and art to select from the total circumstances of a case just what elements are the casual* conditions of learning, which are influential, and which secondary or irrelevant. It requires candor and sincerity to keep track of failures as well as successes and to estimate the relative degree of success obtained. It requires trained and acute observation to note the indications of progress in learning, and even more to detect their causes—a much more highly skilled kind of observation than is needed to note the results of mechanically applied tests. Yet the progress of a science of education depends upon the systematic accumulation of just this sort of material. Solution of the problem of discovering the cause of learning is an endless process. But no advance will be made in the solution till a start is made, and the freer and more experimental character of progressive schools places the responsibility for making the start squarely upon them.

I hardly need remind you that I have definitely limited the field of discussion to one point: the relation of progressive education to the development of a science of education. As I began with questions, I end with one: Is not the time here when the progressive movement is sufficiently established so that it may now consider the intellectual contribution which it may make to the art of education, to the art which is the most difficult and the most important of all human arts?

* Causal? *M.S.D.*

Introduction

BY JOHN DEWEY

to *The Use of Resources in Education**

BY ELSIE RIPLEY CLAPP

◆

*Dewey's last published work on education was this
introduction to a book by a former student and
Assistant in his courses in philosophy of education
at Teachers College, Columbia University. The
book, published for The John Dewey Society, is "an
account of the use and development in education
of the resources children and their families use daily
as they live. . . ." focusing on two public rural schools
in Kentucky and West Virginia respectively. Dewey
used the introduction as an opportunity to review
his association of over half a century with the progressive education movement. Here, at the very close
of his career, remembering his hopes for the progressive idea, he reveals a profound disappointment over
what the movement had become, and a sad concern
over what it might yet be.*

The invitation of the John Dewey Society to write something by way of introduction to Miss Clapp's account of
two important educational experiments is an honor and
also something of an embarrassment. It is an honor to
become associated, however indirectly, with the ground-
breaking educational undertakings which are here re-

* New York: Harper & Brothers, 1952, copyright 1952 by Elsie
Ripley Clapp. Introduction reprinted by permission of Harper &
Brothers.

ported by the one who was largely responsible for in-
itiating them. The invitation is an embarrassment because Miss Clapp has not only given a full, vivid and
convincing description of the practical phases of the
work, what was done and how; she has also given a clear
and illuminating interpretation of its theoretical content
and meaning: the purposes that inspired it, the leading
principles that guided it, the educational philosophy of
which it is an expression and embodiment. It would be
to engage in a wholly superfluous performance if I were
to detain the reader with any restatement of the basic
ideas Miss Clapp has so effectively stated in the context
of describing the educational work actually done, where
the ideas take on life and their consequences become
manifest.

But it may not be altogether superfluous for me to say
something about the whole educational movement of
which the work here described and interpreted is a part.
This seems to me all the more appropriate to do because
the work which is the occasion for my remarks concretely
exemplifies, in my judgment, what is most valuable in
the movement.

In the course of more than half a century of participation in the theory and practice of education, I have witnessed many successes and many failures in what is most
popularly known as "progressive education," but is also
known as "the new education," "modern education," and
so on. These designations are singular but they cover a
plurality of different movements which have in common
the general objective of improving the educational system but which differ from one another in many specific
respects—ideas, principles, policies and programs. The
confusion in public discussion of educational problems
does not arise from using the term "progressive education" instead of "new education" or vice versa. It arises
from using these designations as if they were proper
names, denoting a singular entity. This is hardly the
place to enter into terminological problems; however, it
is in place to point out that I shall use the designations
"progressive education" and "the progressive education

movement" as common names, that is, as convenient linguistic means of referring to the whole complex of diversified movements and efforts to improve the practice and theory of education.

During the past few years, organized attacks on the achievements of progressive education have become more extensive and virulent than ever before. The current effort to turn the clock back in education is a real cause for alarm but not for surprise. The educational system is part of the common life and cannot escape suffering the consequences that flow from the conditions prevailing outside the school building. When repressive and reactionary forces are increasing in strength in all our other institutions—economic, social and political—it would be folly to expect the school to get off free.

For the same reason, it is folly to think that the progressive education movement was something thought up and put over by the teachers all by themselves. On the intellectual side, it was part of the wider movement of thought, the inquiries into the nature and problems of growth which constitute the great contribution of the second half of the nineteenth century to the advancement of human knowledge in the biological, psychological and sociological sciences. On the social side, it was part of the widespread effort to liberate individuals and institutions from bondage to repressive modes of life. Without the support of the progressive and enlightening forces in the community, intellectual and social, the teachers of new vision would have been at best like Arnold's Shelley, ineffectual angels, born out of their time, and all their best plans and ideas would have had little or no effect on the educational system.

The most widespread and marked success of the progressive education movement has been in bringing about a significant change in the life-conditions in the classroom. There is a greater awareness of the needs of the growing human being, and the personal relations between teachers and students have been to a noticeable extent humanized and democratized. But the success in these respects is as yet limited; it is largely atmospheric;

it hasn't yet really penetrated and permeated the foundations of the educational institution. The older gross manifestations of the method of education by fear and repression—physical, social and intellectual—which was the established norm for the educational system before the progressive education movement began have, generally speaking, been eliminated. But the basic attitudes underlying the gross manifestations have in many areas still to be rooted out. The fundamental authoritarianism of the old education persists in various modified forms. There is a great deal of talk about education being a cooperative enterprise in which teachers and students participate democratically, but there is far more talk about it than the doing of it. To be sure, many teachers, particularly in the kindergarten and elementary schools, take the children into sharing with them to an extent impossible and inconceivable under the old system whose supreme achievement of educational wisdom is enshrined in its maxim: spare the rod and spoil the child.

In the secondary schools and colleges, however, there isn't much sharing on the part of teachers in the needs and concerns of those whom they teach. Of course, the conditions still too largely prevailing in the school—the size of the classes, the load of work, and so on—make it difficult to carry on the educative process in any genuinely cooperative, democratic way. These conditions, however, are not the sole causes for the failures in educational democracy, as is evident from the fact that in "progressive" schools where these deplorable conditions do not exist education as thoroughgoing sharing is often rather more a theme of discourse in various courses in the curriculum than a practice observable in the conduct of the school. What it really means to make the educative process a genuine sharing, a truly cooperative transaction in which both teachers and students engage as equals and learners is demonstrated in the cases Miss Clapp describes. Nothing I can say in amplification of this point would add to what the reader will find abundantly illustrated in this work.

It should be a commonplace, but unfortunately it is not, that no education—or anything else for that matter —is progressive unless it is making progress. Nothing is more reactionary in its consequences than the effort to live according to the ideas, principles, customs, habits or institutions which at some time in the past represented a change for the better but which in the present constitute factors in the problems confronting us. The fact that a given change was made in order to realize a desirable end in view signifies that the life-conditions before and after are different. In the process of attaining that good, a new situation was created. A new complex of life-conditions was brought into existence presenting its own distinctive characteristics and problems. Blind attachment to what was good for a state of affairs that no longer exists prevents recognition of the needs of the present and blots out of view the desirable ends that those needs should generate. As Emerson puts it, the attained good tends to become the enemy of the better.

New problems cannot be met intelligently by routine application of ideas and principles which were developed in solving different problems. New problems demand for their intelligent solution the projection of new purposes, new ends in view; and new ends necessitate the development of new means and methods. Of course, the "new" is, in all cases, relatively, not absolutely, new. Even though something absolutely new may be desirable, and some may delude themselves into thinking they have something absolutely new, the continuities in culture and experience exclude the possibility of anything having in fact this absolute character. The danger of cutting through all relations and connections inherited from the past is purely chimerical. The real danger is in perpetuating the past under forms that claim to be new but are only disguises of the old.

What has just been said is illustrated in the history of the progressive education movement—as in every other area of human effort and advance. It accounts for the failure in the movement which can no more be attributed to the teachers alone than can its successes. To change long-established habits in the individual is a slow, difficult and complicated process. To change long-established institutions—which are social habits organized in the structure of the common life—is a much slower, more difficult and far more complicated process. The drive of established institutions is to assimilate and distort the new into conformity with themselves. This drive or tendency in the educational institution is perhaps most glaringly evident in the way the ideas and principles of the educational philosophy I have had a share in developing are still for the most part taught, more than half a century after they began to find their way in various parts of the school. In teachers colleges and elsewhere the ideas and principles have been converted into a fixed subject matter of ready-made rules, to be taught and memorized according to certain standardized procedures and, when occasion arises, to be applied to educational problems externally, the way mustard plasters, for example, are applied.

In other words, habits of "learning" institutionalized and perpetuated for centuries seek to transform into their own image ideas and principles which explicitly emphasize that learning is a method of growth and that the educative process does not consist in acquiring a kit of tools but is a process of learning means and methods of human growth which can never be fixed but must be constantly developed for the intelligent solution of new problems or more adequate solution of old problems partially solved. Considered from the most general philosophical point of view, this conversion—or perversion—of means and methods into a fixed, self-sufficient subject matter is due to the persistence and power of the traditional notion that the qualities of ideas are inherent, eternal and immutable essences. On this theory, the principles of progressive education (of whatever sort they may be) are "inherently progressive" and anyone who can recite them is *ipso facto* a "progressive" teacher.

It may perhaps be said that to train teachers in the right principles the wrong way is an improvement over teacher-training that is wrong in both respects. But it is not much of an improvement. For the *method* of training—inside or outside the school—forms character. The *method* of teacher-training in teachers colleges is not of course the sole determinant of the characters of the future teachers; but in so far as the method of training is successful it forms their character *as teachers,* and hence is a significant determinant of their moral development. Training in the right principles the wrong way means in effect to create a split between the moral and intellectual training of teachers. The principles they learn to recite acquire the function of a verbal veneer. To the extent that their training is effective and until it is modified (for better or worse) by post-training experiences, they will teach as they were taught in fact, not as they were taught *about* teaching as a subject of educational theory.

Speaking again from the most general philosophical standpoint, this authoritarian principle in education and the consequences that flow from it in the conduct of the school will never be effectively eradicated as long as the traditional notion prevails that the qualities of ideas are inherent essences. For it follows from this notion or doctrine that the education of teachers consists in transmitting to them certain collections of fixed, immutable subject matter which they in turn are to transmit to the students under them. The educational regimen thus consists of authorities at the upper end handing down to the receivers at the lower end what they must accept. This is not education but indoctrination, propaganda. It is a type of "education" fit for the foundations of a totalitarian society and, for the same reason, fit to subvert, pervert and destroy the foundations of a democratic society.

For the creation of a democratic society we need an educational system where the process of moral-intellectual development is in practice as well as in theory a cooperative transaction of inquiry engaged in by free, independent human beings who treat ideas and the heritage of the past as means and methods for the further enrichment of life, quantitatively and qualitatively, who use the good attained for the discovery and establishment of something better.

But I fear I have already detained the reader too long from making first-hand acquaintance with Miss Clapp's stimulating and illuminating account of practical demonstrations of the good that has been attained by the progressive education movement and of the better that is to come.